All Roads Lead To Jerusalem

Jerusalem

"The Aliyah Story"

By Harriot Hayes

All Roads lead To Jerusalem, "The Aliyah Story"
By Harriot Hayes

Copyright © 2010 by Harriot Hayes.
ISBN: 978-1-257-26033-1

About The Cover

The Picture:

A windmill set atop the ageless city whose entryway is depicted by two ancient gates, this is the artist's simple rendition of Jerusalem. The Yemin Moshe windmill, built by the British Jewish philanthropist Moses Montefiore in 1857, was erected to encourage and service the first 19th century Jewish settlement built outside the Jerusalem Old City walls. In many ways, the Montefiore windmill became a symbol of the anticipated establishment of modern day Israel which occurred in 1948. When I arrived in Jerusalem in 1998, some 50 years later, I was drawn to this windmill. It had a kind of prophetic significance for me. And so for a season I would stand atop a high rock next to the windmill to join in with the proclamation of the Old Testament prophet, Ezekiel, as I called forth the Jews of the nations to return to their God-given Homeland:

... "Prophesy to the breath, prophesy, son of man, and say to the breath, 'Thus says the Lord God: "Come from the four winds, O breath, and breath on these slain, that they may live." '"
(Ezekiel 37:9)

Though this act might seem silly or even bizarre to some, I knew that as I agreed with the Word of God, spoken so long ago through the mouth of the ancient prophet, that a proclamation would go forth to the 'four winds' as I faced first north, then south, east, and west, calling the Jewish people Home to Israel. Interestingly enough, the same Hebrew word (ruach) is used for WIND, BREATH/or 'to breathe', and SPIRIT as in Holy Spirit! The 'slain' of verse 9 (above) are the 'dry bones' that come to life and the 'whole house of Israel' according to the two following verses, (10 & 11). "Oh, that they may live", says the prophet! In Isaiah, another Old Testament prophetic book, the Lord speaks to Israel:

iii

Fear not, for I am with you; I will bring your descendents from the east, and gather you from the west; I will say to the north, 'Give them up!' And to the south, 'Do not keep them back!' Bring My sons from afar, and My daughters from *the ends of the earth...*

(Isaiah 43:5 & 6)

The Subtitle: THE ALIYAH STORY

For many the word ALIYAH is unfamiliar. In the Hebrew language this word is formed from the three letter root in the verb, (la'alot) meaning 'to go up'. Biblically speaking, this is always the way one goes to Jerusalem. You never go 'down' to Jerusalem, but you go UP to Jerusalem! Thus the more modern designation of ALIYAH is used to describe Jews from the nations who immigrate to Israel. They talk about making aliyah to Israel. Central to the picture are two roads leading up to two open gates. The road to the right is etched with the word 'Russia', and the map fragments depicting Georgia and Armenia; these are all countries that the writer has had the joy and privilege of visiting to assist with God's aliyah directive. Many Jews have returned to Israel from these nations lying to Israel's north, (Russia & the old Soviet Bloc countries), and just to the east of Israel (Georgia & Armenia). Though some will continue to make 'aliyah' from these areas, I believe that the heavenly spotlight is now turning to the WEST. Europe and North America, especially the United States with an estimated Jewish population of more than six million, is about to get a wake-up call...................but I'm getting ahead of myself here! (You'll have to read on to get 'the rest of the story'). Regarding aliyah, my earnest prayer and hope in making my story available is two-fold: first, that God's vision for aliyah would be etched in the hearts of my Christian readers, beckoning them to assist their Jewish friends and neighbors to fulfill the Biblical directive of the second Exodus return to Israel, and second, that our Jewish brethren would be stirred from deep within to make Eretz Israel their HOME.

TABLE OF CONTENTS

PART II: Russia, a 'Spiritual' Travelogue

PART III: All Roads Lead To Jerusalem

Dedication

This book is dedicated to all of the special men and women along the way who have been a part of this story. I can't give their actual names but as they read this book they will know who they are, and without a doubt, the wonderful God we serve knows exactly who they are! I praise God for each one who has walked a segment of the journey with me. Whether serving quietly 'backstage' in a supportive role or functioning in a more frontal position, their impact on God's maidservant and His Kingdom work has not gone unnoticed. Here I want to especially lift up Amari and his wife who, along with their congregation and staff, carried out the precious aliyah work on the Black Sea coast and neighboring Armenia and Georgia. I know that their unselfish service to the Jewish people was dear to the Father's heart. Finally, I want to make special mention of the sacrifice that my daughter Alice has made in letting her mother walk out the pages of this book in faraway lands. It hasn't been easy for her, or her mother for that matter, but God provided His best help in the person of my sister 'Regina' to fill in during my absences. Regina has always faithfully been there to pick up the slack as 'mom', 'aunt grammie' to my grandchildren, and 'editor & chief', taking care of all the necessary business there so that I could be free to function overseas. I continue to tell her that any fruit borne is credited equally to her heavenly account as well. My deepest thanks and appreciation go out to all of these dear saints who have walked the various parts of this spiritual journey with me!

ALL ROADS LEAD TO JERUSALEM

"One ordinary woman's account of her journey with God Who led her from Moscow to Jerusalem and beyond!"

"INTRODUCTION"

Children have a natural ability, I think, to tap into that supernatural realm that Jesus so often spoke about, the "Kingdom of God". Perhaps it's because they haven't become fully programmed yet to navigate their way through life according to what we adults call 'reality'. Or maybe it's simply because they are born with a keen awareness of His Presence, an awareness which will eventually fade as they are taught to focus on the more tangible and natural world.

I can remember a number of encounters with His supernatural Presence during my earliest years, long before the "cares of this world" tried to snuff out His candle within me. Many nights, I would lay in bed and imagine being with Jesus as His Holy Spirit enveloped me. Sometimes, I would experience vivid dreams that depicted angels and the gardens of heaven. But the most wonderful dream that I can recall was my "Jacob's ladder" dream. I'm not exactly sure how old I was when this dream occurred, probably somewhere between the ages of three and five, but I know that it was long before I knew about the account of Jacob's dream in Genesis 28. In this, my child's dream, I got to actually climb the ladder that connected earth with heaven. I saw the angels busily descending and ascending the steps of the ladder, but my dream ended before I was able to slip through heaven's portal. I could only see it from the top of the ladder though I felt the Presence of God intensely indwelling what Jacob identified as "the gateway to heaven". And so as a very young child, God and His supernatural realm were as real to me as the natural world I had been born into.

I don't want to dwell too long on this initial part of my journey other than to make the point that from birth, indeed from the womb, there is something lodged down deep within our souls that cries out for God's Presence. We are more aware of this during our first years of life, before an estrangement from God follows at the heels of childhood innocence. The end result is a wandering soul who is left unfulfilled and incomplete because he yearns for the One who created him and gave him life in the first place. It doesn't matter how rich or successful he is by the world's standards or how highly esteemed he may be. There will always be an empty void that only God can fill.

And so this is why I believe the Holy Spirit is instructing me to write this book, so that I can be a testimony, a testimony of one ordinary woman who has pursued God with all of her heart! As I have determined to put Him at the very center of my life, He has met me every step of the way and rewarded my obedience to follow Him. But this walk of obedience and faith did not occur until everything in my life had seemingly come crashing down upon me. Only then did a very crucial transition begin to take place within me as I earnestly turned to God after the termination of a devastating marriage.

I could write volumes about what happened during this time, but it's not my desire to dwell on the enemy's works, but rather on the Lord's. To give the reader just a bit of background, I will share that only a couple of weeks before our marriage, the young man who had become my husband during our college years, had taken a strong hallucinatory drug called LSD. He was never right after this and there were multiple episodes of manic-depressive and schizophrenic behavior that followed. This kind of bondage, I now recognize, has its spiritual roots embedded in the kingdom of darkness. But back then, I wasn't spiritually equipped to understand this. All I knew was that I had become a prisoner of fear and hopelessness. I honestly can't recall any good memories that arose out of our 5½ years of marriage other than, of course, our daughter, Alice. This all happened during the 70's. It was at this horrible time in my life that I remembered the Jesus of my tender youth. I cried out to Him from my heart and challenged Him to help turn my life around saying, "If You're real, show Yourself to me!" In my own simple but honest way, I repented for my rebellion and for making such a mess of things. I can recall the feeling of peace and lightness that followed. It was as if a great burden had been lifted from me.

My real journey had just now begun. It would promise to be a journey that would lead me to many new places and situations. Along the way, there would always be lessons to be learned as well as times of serious testing, but ultimately, from all of this, the end result would be a deeper knowledge of God and His ways.

For I know the thoughts that I think toward you, says the Lord, thoughts of peace and not of evil, to give you a future and a hope. Then you will call upon Me and go and pray to Me, and I will listen to you. And you will seek Me and find Me, when you search for Me with all your heart. I will be found by you, says the Lord, and I will bring you back from your captivity; (Jeremiah 29: 11-14a)

"A NOTE FROM THE AUTHOR"

I would ask the reader to please be aware that in most cases the names of individuals, who became part of my journey, have been changed. Also, any direct references to organizations or groups have been avoided. In an effort to protect God's work that is ongoing, locations of various ministries may be generalized. Finally, I too must operate under the covering of a 'ghost writer' pen name as God's current 'Kingdom business' in my life necessitates this.

I pray that in some special way the sharing of my journey with you, the reader, will encourage and bless you! For those who have not yet met the God of Abraham and His Promised Messiah, Jesus, I pray that this humble testimony will make you want to know Him. For those of you who have wondered if there's more to God than what you've experienced in your life thus far, I pray that the Holy Spirit will nudge you forward in your walk with Him, causing you to press in ever deeper to really know Him. And for those who seem to be stuck in the midst of spiritual battles and tests, I pray that somehow the truth will emerge that through determined 'faith and patience', God will bring successively greater victories into your life. With each test successfully completed and each battle won, our vessel becomes more refined in the Holy fires. Not only that, but a greater measure of faith emerges, a faith that has the potential to open wide the door into His Kingdom Realm. From this, our vantage point with the King, nothing is impossible!

His servant and one of the sheep,
Harriot Hayes

PART I

The Journey Begins

Chapter One

"Boston, 'Human' Angels, & the Holy Spirit"

I couldn't believe that I was actually in Boston and ready to begin classes at one well-known denominational seminary. As I looked at all the boxes and furniture piled high inside my small studio apartment, I marveled that God had made it possible, against great odds, for me to be there. He had provided full tuition and a part time job; I only had to believe him for part of my living expenses. This was a gigantic step of faith for me back then, but I had just come out of such bedlam in my life that I was nearly ready to try anything new that seemed plausible to achieve. As strange as it may sound, for some reason, God had put this thought into my heart, that I should become a minister in a church. Now I know that this is not the norm for women and I would view this whole matter in quite a different light today, but back then, it made sense to me. And honestly speaking, I can look back at these three years in Boston now and see the hand of God mightily at work, in this, the beginning chapter of my walk with Him. Little Alice, of course, came with me. Boston would also prove to be a whole new experience for her.

As I started the monumental task of unpacking boxes, my thoughts drifted back to the past year. Only one year had elapsed since my separation and divorce. It had not been an easy year to say the least! During this time, Alice and I had lived with Regina, my older sister and her daughter, Ann, who was four. We all lived in an upstairs apartment that belonged to our parents. Mom and Dad lived under us with our younger sister, Ruth, and our elderly grandmother. What made it especially difficult was that Alice, my three and a half year-old, was having a terrible time adjusting to this new living situation. As a result, she and her cousin, Ann, became both the best of friends and the worst of enemies during this time, perhaps acting more like rivaling sisters than cousins. (In fact, to this day, they would consider themselves the closest of sisters, but, "Praise God", without the battles of the earlier days!) It was God's blessing for me at the beginning of this time that I had quickly landed a good job doing counseling and outreach work with young pregnant teens. This position, with a religious adoption agency in town, was demanding of my time and definitely stretched my abilities to deal with crisis situations, but it helped me to take my focus off from my own problems and to concentrate more on assisting these young girls. As I look back, somehow going through their fires with them helped me to more easily go through my own fires.

Most of my days at the seminary were very busy. Trying to be a full time graduate student and mother was plenty to handle, but at one point, I was also traveling to a nearby town several days a week to do my internship at a local church. And to fill my plate just a bit more, I still had the part time job to keep up with! At the end of each semester, I can remember marathon nights when I would stay up late and get up very early the next morning in order to turn out required term papers and study for exams. How I ever got through it all, the Lord only knows, but somehow He gave me the grace, not only do it, but to have some measure of success in the process.

The courses that were offered were, for the most part, 'heady', that is to say, they took on a very intellectual approach to God. During lectures, the God of the Bible was 'analyzed', 'philosophized', and the Truth of His Word was 'scrutinized', yet no professor there, except possibly one Old Testament professor, seemed to really know God. That was what I was hungry for, the knowledge of God! But in spite of all this, during my first year as a student, I wasn't dissatisfied with the liberal curriculum. Still a youngster in the Lord and basically yet untaught in His ways, I was just 'bubbling' along with excitement and looking for something or someone to grab onto who could open up the reality of a personal God to me. The Lord knew my hunger in this regard and so He appointed one special couple, I believe, to enroll at the seminary.

To this day, I think that they still wonder how they ended up at this particular seminary as it was totally out of line with their own experiences in the Lord. I used to tell them that they had been sent there because of me. And do you know what? My Heavenly Father loved me so much that this may very well have been the case! He wanted to quench some of my thirst for Him and to introduce me to His Living Presence. So in order to do that, it took the right 'living vessels' and the drawing of His Spirit. This time God sent me some 'human' Angels!

Jeff and Betty Angel, a couple from the Midwest, enrolled in the sacred music department at the seminary some time during my second year there. Because I sang in the student choir, I started to become acquainted with Jeff who was doing his student internship in choral directing with our group. His wife, Betty, also sang with us. There was something about this couple that really drew me to them, something that I had never previously noticed in another person. I couldn't put my finger on it at first, but whenever I was around them the spirit within me would begin to stir. Little did I know at the time that this 'charismatic' couple had somehow found their way into this very liberal seminary and that their presence there would cause a significant transformation in my walk with the Lord.

By the beginning of my last year of seminary, I was growing weary of living in the middle of a big city. Besides that, there had been too much loud partying going on in our student apartment building to make it conducive for studying. It was then, in the fall of 1980, that some of the theology students decided to join forces and resources to procure housing together in a nearby suburb. Originally, this plan to move and share housing started out with a small group of us, but in the end only Alice and I plus the Angels were left. As Jeff, Betty and I discussed this, we decided to still go ahead with the plan. By this time, we had begun to get to know each other and so for a year or so, we felt that the pooling of resources could provide a much more pleasant living situation. The house that we rented in Weston was spacious and brand new. We shared the kitchen and living room and some meals together while each of us went about our busy lives with school and work.

A couple of weeks after moving in, the Angels decided to have several friends over on a Thursday evening for a prayer meeting. At first when they tried to include me in this, I wanted to find a way to gracefully decline because I wasn't quite sure what it would be all about. You see, to this point, my understanding of prayer and prayer meetings was lacking, essentially because I had never been around people who really had a relationship with the Lord and therefore knew how to pray from their hearts based on that relationship! The tradition of the denominational church that I had been raised in was basically void of a prayer life other than the prayers on Sunday mornings that the minister had composed earlier on and read from a piece of paper. Likewise, he also offered prayers from the back of the congregational hymnal, but somehow these prayers had always seemed empty to me. And so, I had never been to a real prayer meeting, but because I resided in the same house that the prayer meeting was to take place, there was little room for escape. Of course, God had set this whole thing up, and so I rather cautiously walked into His Divine trap!

Thursday evening arrived, and so did Jeff and Betty's friends. I found out later that they had all come to Boston not only from the same state, but also with connections to the same church! As we settled into our chairs that had been arranged in a circle in the living room, Jeff pulled out his guitar and a few simple songs to the Lord were sung:

"Jesus, Jesus, Jesus, there's just something about Your Name, Master, Savoir, Jesus, like the spring time after the rain..."

There it was again! 'Something' wonderful started to stir inside of me and I knew that it had to do with the Lord. And then as we held hands and the others quietly prayed under their breath, I could

10

sense little gentle waves of Divine electricity. As I questioned what this was, I listened more closely to their prayers. They were not speaking English or any other language that I had ever heard before. I noted that each one prayed differently. Sometimes their prayer language flowed with a kind of lilt to it, and at other times, a particular pattern of words would develop. They spoke ever so softly and tenderly and so I didn't find this offensive at all. On the contrary, there was such a heavenly peace in the room that it was almost as if they were speaking these words to God Himself, and as I learned later on, indeed they were!

I couldn't wait until the following Friday morning to talk to my friend, Lindsey, about what had happened. After all, I thought, she's a minister's daughter and she should know something about this! Sure enough, she did, though not on a personal level. As I explained about the strange words being uttered and the events of the previous evening, she paused for a moment and then offered an explanation. "I think that this was 'speaking in other tongues' ", she said, "you know, something like what happened in the book of Acts, chapter 2."

Well, that was about all that I could glean from Lindsey, and I had to admit, that I was only vaguely familiar with the story of Pentecost back then. What little I did know about supernatural manifestations seemed confined to the times of Jesus and His disciples in the context of the events of the New Testament. I had never imagined that such things could really happen today! I pulled out my Bible and reviewed Acts, chapter 2. There I began reading about the disciples who had 'tarried' in Jerusalem as Jesus had commanded them to do. I pondered about what had really taken place when they were filled with the Holy Spirit and spoke in other tongues. In his discourse on this most unique day of Pentecost, Peter gave full explanation of the whole phenomena of the strange tongues that the bewildered feast goers, mainly Jews from other lands, had just witnessed:

For these are not drunk, as you suppose, since it is only the third hour of the day. But this is what was spoken by the prophet Joel: 'And it shall come to pass in the last days, says God, That I will pour out of My Spirit on all flesh; Your sons and your daughters shall prophesy, Your young men shall see visions, Your old men shall dream dreams. And on My menservants and on My maidservants I will pour out My Spirit in those days; And they shall prophesy.' (Acts 2:15-18)

I made my way to verses 38 and 39 of that same chapter:

Then Peter said to them, "Repent, and let every one of you be baptized in the name of Jesus Christ for the remission of sins; and you shall receive the gift of the Holy Spirit. For the promise is to you and to your children, and to all who are afar off, as many as the Lord our God will call." (Acts 2:38 & 39)

This statement about the 'promise' seemed to be pretty universal, spanning both time and the various people groups. I noted also that Jesus Himself referred to the 'promise' of receiving the Holy Spirit in the last chapter of the Gospel of Luke. These were some of His parting words to His disciples just before being taken up into heaven:

"Behold, I send the Promise of My Father upon you; but tarry in the city of Jerusalem until you are endued with power from on high." (Luke 24:49)

This time the word 'Promise' was capitalized! By the end of my search, I understood that the Promise of being filled with the Holy Spirit was available to me also and that one would be empowered with God's manifest Presence when such an event occurred. The idea of speaking in a supernatural language intrigued me, but what impacted me even more was the possibility that I could experience the very Presence of the Lord that I had been hungering for all these years. With each passing thought, my God was becoming more real and alive to me. More than anything, I wanted His Spirit to indwell my little temple! My thoughts raced ahead further to what this all really meant. I started to understand that the miracles of God that had occurred at the hands of Jesus and his disciples were possible today! As I pondered all of this, a great excitement began to build up inside of me. Another simple, but very sincere prayer emerged from my lips, (not unlike the one that I had prayed just three years ago asking Jesus to come into my life), "God, if all of this is real, I want it! I want to be filled with Your Holy Spirit. I want to pray in tongues and to speak to You in a heavenly language."

The next Thursday evening was only a day away! The Angels and their friends had decided to get together weekly for prayer, and so I was looking forward to this second meeting. All week, I had been so busy with my classes and work that there was little room for anything else to occupy my time but by Wednesday my thoughts began to focus back to the events of the prior Thursday evening. What would take place during this second prayer meeting will be indelibly marked in my memory because it was during this second Thursday in October of 1980 that the Holy Spirit came upon me in a mighty way. In fact, I had already had this experience of being baptized in the Spirit the night before in a very vivid dream. But now, what had been ordained in the heavenly realm was about to become manifest in my everyday life.

I can remember sitting down to join our little group of five or six. I had just completed another busy day and hadn't yet shaken off the 'cares of the world' so that I could turn my attention more fully on the Lord. Despite this, almost immediately as I sat down a rush of His Presence hit me. We began to praise and worship the Lord while this sensation of the Spirit of God only intensified. I don't think that anyone there was aware of what was happening to me as I struggled to contain myself. Literally, I could feel the Presence of God filling me, indeed saturating my very being! The strangest sensation began to take over my mouth and tongue. I don't know how else to describe it, but there was a great force and pressure that seemed to rise up out of my 'belly' and exert itself on my oral mechanism. Marvelous words that I had never heard or spoken before began to fill my spirit and mind. As if the whole manifestation hadn't been strong enough, the Holy Spirit directed Jeff to come over to me a short time after this had all started. He laid his hands on my head and prayed for the Lord to fill me. The result was that my already filled condition now became that of overflowing and I truly thought that I was going to pass out. I didn't understand a thing back then about yielding to the Spirit of God or what some call 'resting in the Spirit', and so I fought this sensation with everything that was within me. Now of course, the Lord could have totally wiped me out on the living room floor and caused me to release the flow that was ready to explode within me. But, 'Praise God', He knew that up until this point of my life, my reserved and somewhat shy nature couldn't handle a public display of my new prayer language. And so I somehow managed to contain it all until the prayer time had ended and I was able to go into my bedroom alone and shut the door behind me. There, alone with my God, I opened my mouth and marveled as the most glorious flood of words emerged from my spirit.

The days that followed my experience were intense and wonderful. I felt as though a new dimension had been added to my life. The only way I can describe it is that before being baptized in the Holy Spirit, I felt like a flat two-dimensional picture. After the experience, I felt three-dimensional. Perhaps that was because I could actually feel the Spirit of God dwelling within me and with me. For several weeks, I had all that I could do to contain myself. The desire to pray in the Spirit, that is to say, with my new prayer language, was ever present. I did a lot of walking back then to get to classes or to pick Alice up from school or the sitters and I can remember just walking about the city praying and singing in my heavenly language, almost totally oblivious to what was going on around me. If anyone had heard me, they probably would have thought that I was a little bit crazy, but I didn't really care. I just wanted to be in His Holy Presence, and so back then, we had sweet times of fellowship on the streets of Boston.

Another thing that resulted from all this was my desire to tell everyone about what had happened to me. I wanted them to know that God was alive and very real, not just some distant Being that we religiously pray to, and at best, only expect to meet in some afterlife. No, they needed to know that He is a Living God who wants to touch us today with His miracles and His Presence. In my boldness and zeal to get the word out, I found myself in a number of uneasy situations, chief among them being my disclosure about what had happened to me to the pastor of the church where I had been an intern. In my naiveté, I had thought that he would be excited and would also want to receive this glorious gift that Jesus had promised to the believers. Instead, I observed his countenance harden while I spoke about my Acts chapter 2 experience. His response was a stern warning to me about those who had claimed this kind of experience. "They have caused many problems including church splits", he cautioned me. I cringed inside as the reality hit me that the Holy Spirit in all His fullness would not always be welcome!

In May 1981, I completed my seminary training. It was at this time that the Lord put me to my first real test of obedience. I had been offered a full scholarship to work on a doctorate in ministry. My parents, who had steered clear of the local church and anything that smote of religion, were excited that someone in the family might earn a doctorate level degree, even if it was a 'religious' degree! I especially wanted to please my father by accomplishing this. Somehow, I felt that by earning this degree, I would at last earn his love. In addition to this, I was beginning to get 'wet feet' about serving as a minister in a church. I knew that the governing body of my denomination was expecting me to immediately fill a pulpit as soon as I graduated. But deep down inside, I understood that controversy would be my constant companion if I took a church and presented the Real Jesus, (Who I

15

was just getting acquainted with myself), to the people. Clearly, the Lord made it known to me what I needed to do. Anything less would be disobedience. I was to put my personal aspirations aside regarding this additional degree and take the charge that would be offered to me. I knew that the Lord would be with me to walk me through this new adventure. But little did I realize the price that I would have to pay in order to remain faithful to Him and to present the real Gospel to the flock I would be assigned to.

Chapter Two

"No Compromise!"

It was the later part of May 1981 and a gorgeous late spring day. I had just been appointed by my denomination to serve the Lakeland United Church that was located in the foothills of a scenic New England mountain range. A number of little towns were quietly tucked away in this region of lakes, summer guests, and hard-working country folk. My assignment was to fill the pulpit that served two of these towns, Center Lakeland and Lakeland South. The good part for me was that I was given a one-point charge, meaning that the minister didn't have to go to two, three, or even four different church locations to conduct services on Sunday. Most of the new seminary graduates were given these multiple-charges because the minister's salary was lower than what was offered by some of the more prosperous one-church appointments. As a newcomer in my denominational conference, the Lakeland United Church was considered to be a prize appointment. A serious drawback I would soon learn, though, was that a historical division had existed between the two towns, each of which had it's own church building!

To help the reader better understand the challenges that awaited me, I need to explain to you that Lakeland South was considered to be a more 'lower class' town by the citizens of Center Lakeland. As it happened, the church folks in Lakeland South were affiliated with my denomination. Center Lakeland prided itself on being more 'uptown'; their church represented a different Protestant denomination that was somewhat theologically compatible with my denomination, but different in governmental structure, and perhaps a bit more liberal as well. This church grouping voted on and chose their own ministers, giving them much more local control and autonomy, whereas my denomination appointed ministers from their regional conference. Each time a change in clergy was to take place, the two churches would take turns in securing a minister from their respective denomination.

Typical of many areas in New England, both of these towns were proud of their beautiful white church buildings which dated back to the early eighteen hundreds. Many families that I served could trace the establishment of their home church to family members in previous generations. And so, the 'church buildings' had become a very precious symbol to them. It was all very idyllic, white steeples protruding heavenward encased the large brass bells which welcomed the faithful each Sunday morning. I noted that these same bells had rung throughout their respective communities for years! And probably for years also, church goers had a certain expectation about what was to take place inside the church building! There was a particular, familiar structure and format that had to be followed, not to mention a strict time limit set on the length of the services. I learned very quickly that any violation of the standard worship service would have serious consequences for the minister!

And so this was the setting that the Lord had called me into. This newly Spirit-baptized, green seminary graduate, 'woman' minister had been sent to the Lakeland area to serve these two traditional Protestant churches who did not get along! Not only that, but they lacked knowledge of Who the Holy Spirit was, and sadly had never been taught about the absolute truth of God's Word. For most, Jesus was only a historical figure. Relationship with Him and acknowledging His Lordship in their lives was a foreign concept. My job was to introduce them to the Son of the Living God and draw them into His Presence, not such an easy task to accomplish considering some of the stubborn New Englanders that the Lord had put in my bundle! But I understood their thinking and I was only too familiar with the demeanor of these folks, for after all, I was one of them. And I knew only too well the kind of 'church' they had endured since birth. I, too, week after week, had sat through endless empty sermons and the religious protocol immortalized in the hymnals. But, that was all

18

about to change! They had a choice, to choose 'Life' or to continue with spiritual stagnation and death. God's campaign had begun, and His vessel to head this campaign dug her heels in and prepared for the 'fallout' that would surely come, not necessarily from heaven, but from the 'old' dust covering the sanctuary!

Lest the reader begin to think that I had little compassion for the sheep, I must explain that I understood only too well that this spiritual condition wasn't necessarily their fault! For years they had been preached to by preachers who didn't know the Lord or the power of His Presence in the form of the Holy Spirit. Therefore, it was impossible for these 'men of the cloth' to understand God's Word in the Bible. If you don't really know the Author of the Bible, how can you begin to understand what He spoke through the prophets and anointed men of old? How can you begin to unlock the precious wisdom and secrets of the Bible for the flock? You can't! It's impossible to do because the Word of God must be spiritually discerned with the help of the Spirit of God. Sadly, the flock had been fed with sermons that had little or no Biblical basis. The topics that had dominated the Sunday morning pulpit for years ranged in subject matter from social issues of the day and liberation theology to some 'dry as dust' attempts to portray a Biblical story. How do I know this? I'll tell you how! It's because I grew up listening to this very same kind of sermon for the first twenty some odd years of my life! Did it do me any good? No, it left me spiritually hungry and destitute. But now I had found out the Truth and I desperately wanted to help awaken this flock to the reality of God's Presence and to introduce them to Jesus!

A freshly painted apartment atop an old country library was to serve as the parsonage. It was spacious and comfortable, though the building was very old and a bit rickety! I'll never forget the episode of trying to hoist a very large baby grand piano up one level as it swung out over the exterior staircase. I held my breath until the charming old instrument made its way into my living room. There it would be lovingly surrounded by sheep who had newly learned to yield their hearts and voices in worship to their King. Yes, I remember many precious times of true worship as many newcomers and a few of the 'old comers' were transformed by the sweet Presence of God. Sadly, most of the real worship took place in my living room, but not in the sanctuary! Try as we did to flow with the Spirit in the confines of the church building, we were almost always hindered. Not only were there the physical restrictions imposed on us by the 'board', (don't raise your hands, don't get too loud, don't get too emotional, and above all else, do not even dare to sing or pray in tongues), but there was a major demonic stronghold over these towns. It reeked of religiosity! Had I been more experienced and mature at the time, I would have fought this spirit differently and would not have yielded any ground. But I was a novice myself in many ways and didn't fully know what I was up against. Nonetheless, the Lord did! And it was He, knowing the situation from beginning to end, Who sent me there. One thing I did determine from the start, though, was that I would not compromise on the Word of God. The flock would hear about salvation through the Son of God, relationship with Him, and the necessity to be filled with and directed by the Holy Spirit. It would then be up to them about how they would respond.

I have many special memories of the 3 ½ or so years that I spent in the Lakelands. There was indeed a move of God there, the likes of which the folks in this area had never experienced. And, as is the case in all such stirrings of the Holy Spirit, some are strongly drawn into His Presence while others become repelled. The sheep who were drawn were so hungry for the Word of God that our Bible studies would last five hours or more and we had at least two or three of these sessions a week. Now, when I say "Bible study", I don't mean some dry traditional lesson that is perfectly laid out for you with some man's commentary and explanation telling you what to think. Instead, we just started in with one of the Gospels and took it apart, verse by verse, savoring every word, thought, and revelation. The questions that came from the sheep while we pondered over the verses were often quite penetrating, and so together, we would dig into the Bible itself to find out the answers. This always led us from Genesis to the Book of Revelation and everything in-between.

These Bible marathons usually took place in my kitchen around a large wooden table. When the cold winter winds were blowing and the New England snow banks were piled high with the delightful white stuff, we would huddle around the kitchen table, stoke the old wood stove and put on the coffeepot. Out came the Bibles, a concordance and perhaps a Bible dictionary. The Holy Spirit was always faithful to guide us along the way. After all, He is called the "Teacher", so we were in 'good hands' for our spiritual journey! Many times I can remember getting questions that I could not initially answer, but the Spirit of God would give me revelation, sometimes even as I would open my mouth to begin to give explanation. It was so wonderful. I would just sit back with my students and listen to the Holy Spirit instruct me at the same time as I listened to what He was speaking to my spirit and through my mouth! It really was supernatural instruction.

The core of this group, those who couldn't seem to get enough of the Lord and who loved to be with their fellow sheep, was made up of about eight families. Everyone enjoyed each other so much that they were always doing things together as one big family. At the center of this group was one precious brother who was always trying to get something going: a picnic, a hike, cross-country skiing, or whatever seemed good. For example, one time I can remember going tire-tubing down a mountain river. We went for miles, kids and grown-ups alike. It was such a warm sunny day, and the water was brisk, but not icy cold like it would normally be. I'm sure that we had pizza or some such delight after our run on the river. I had always loved this river; it was the same one that we had traveled to earlier on to do some of the baptisms from our group.

As I recall the baptisms, I can remember the day that I baptized a number of folks at a lake in the center of town. As neither of the two denominations I was appointed by believed in baptism by immersion as symbolic confession of truly receiving Jesus into one's life, this was not too popular with the leadership of the church! So, it not only required some determination on my part to baptize the sheep in this way, but it also took some extra courage for the sheep to publicly profess what they believed. This method of baptism was somewhat tolerated by the church hierarchy for a season, but before long I found myself confronted with being asked to do an infant baptism; that is to say, a kind of baby dedication that took the place of baptism as a public profession of faith. In all good conscience, I could not perform this rite and managed to slide out of it by referring the baby's parents to a retired minister in the area who agreed to do the baptism.

Other theological conflicts followed on the heels of a growing discontent with the "lady minista' "! There was the incident of one influential couple in town who wanted to become members of the Center Lakeland church. I quickly realized after my first session with them discussing their beliefs, that agnosticism and New Age concepts guided their theology. But, because of their financial contributions to the church, it didn't really matter to the church elders if they believed in Jesus or not, despite the fact that the tenets of this denomination were historically Christian. Then there were other problems: I preached too literally from the Bible, I was paying too much attention to the newer sheep and spending all my time with them, I was too charismatic in my approach and with the worship, I had stopped wearing the traditional Sunday vestments, I preached at an area tent revival meeting and visited a neighboring charismatic church on a Sunday evening with our little choir. It didn't matter to my contenders if new people were coming to the church and there was a new excitement about a Living Jesus, nor did it matter that some people were getting healed and filled with the Holy Spirit. The Spirit of God was being welcomed by some folks to do a work in their lives, but others rejected Him as they clung tightly onto their comfortable traditions.

The list of complaints was pretty long and growing. By the time I had been there for about a year and a half, I was called on the carpet by the heads of both denominations. A series of meetings followed that addressed not only the issues of controversy surrounding 'yours truly', but also a reassessment was made of the marriage of convenience between the two churches, that is to say, their sharing of a minister. These were very hard times for me. On the one hand, I was totally unmovable about what I believed to be God's Truth and I had a forehead of flint when it came to defending that Truth. But, on the other hand, I was very sensitive and easily wounded by sharp conversations and arguments. I shed many tears during those several months that the meetings took place. Sometimes it felt like my very insides were going to burst within me, it hurt so much. Even my immediate ministerial overseer tried to reason with me, "Harriot, you need to do what the local leadership wants, after all they are the ones sponsoring your pay check! We are here to serve them you know."

The outcome of these meetings was the recommendation that the two denominations needed to have a peaceful divorce and that the Lakeland South Church would retain me as their minister. I realized that their decision to keep me on had more to do with pride, (because I had been appointed by their denomination), rather than compatibility with the denomination's religious practices; it was a kind of statement the Lakeland South folks wanted to make to the Center Lakeland establishment. I held on for a while, but soon realized that I was being confined to a spiritual box that excluded the true works of God. I could never be what God wanted me to be in such a situation. I knew that the Lord was calling me out of this denominational setting. I gave my notice and asked that my ministerial papers be withdrawn. I was then left praying and wondering what the Lord would do with me next. I had a daughter to support and care for, so of course an income would have to come from somewhere. In giving up my credentials, I was giving up the time and money that had been invested in my education. If I played their game, I could have financial security and a prestigious position. But none of that mattered now. I only wanted to serve my God in integrity and to press in to know Him more.

Chapter Three

"A 'Supernatural' Education"

The Lord had it all worked out for me, as usual, so there was no need to fret about this transition. The faithful part of the flock wanted me to stay in Lakeland South and continue teaching the Bible studies as well as holding Sunday services for them. They didn't want to let go of what the Lord was doing there and neither did I. We all recognized that perhaps the Lord wasn't finished yet with His work and that I needed to remain, at least for a season.

For the first few months, the sheep came together frequently, though informally. We had no official 'title' or church backing until one day when a well-known Pentecostal denomination approached me. They had heard about the stirring of the Holy Spirit in our midst from one pastor in their denomination and wanted to invite our flock to become a 'church planting' missionary project. It was amazing that I was accepted and welcomed by this group as a female pastor! The Lord had given me great favor with the leadership and especially their superintendent. After conferring with the sheep, their invitation was accepted. A special blessing for me in all of this was that I was given a modest salary. And along with that came the love and encouragement of the brethren of this denomination to help move the flock forward.

It was wonderful to feel totally free to flow in the gifts of the Spirit at last! As I look back, I can recognize my immaturity in spiritual matters, but still the Lord honored my zeal for Him and my childlike hunger to see Him visibly move. There were some healings and deliverances that took place, and it was not uncommon to see this one or that one resting on the carpet as they were overcome by the power of the Holy Spirit. There were times when His Presence was so strong that I, myself, could not stir from my chair or the floor, whatever position I found myself in as the Spirit of God began to minister. During those days, I used to pray over almost anything that moved! I had great faith, (though it was an immature, undeveloped faith back then), to see the sick healed, the prisoners set free and the broken-hearted restored to wholeness in Him. Isaiah 61:1 was my theme song, and indeed it continues to be:

"The Spirit of the Lord God is upon Me,
Because the Lord has anointed Me
To preach good tidings to the poor;
He has sent me to heal the brokenhearted,
To proclaim liberty to the captives,
And the opening of the prison to those who are bound;"

You might complain that this Scripture applies only to the Messiah, but I must tell you that we are the Body of Messiah, commissioned to carry on His works as we are enabled by His Spirit to crush the works of the powers of darkness. The Kingdom of God is not going to just appear one day without our active participation to overcome the enemy. It was Jesus' full intention and purpose to usher in victory for God's Kingdom through His redeemed body of believers! If you are walking in faith with Him, that's you!

And so to continue with this theme, as I reflect back there were times that the spiritual dimension that I was being caught up in became so intense that I would just have to pull myself away and do some normal every day activities. Baking cookies or walking around a shopping mall, for example, would give me temporary relief. I would react differently to all of this today, of course, considering that the feeling of being overwhelmed had much to do with my 'youth' in the things of God. At any rate, this 'supernatural education' was moving along at a very fast pace. I struggled to keep up, while at the same time I determined to keep pressing forward with My God. There would be no turning back!

One of the more notable episodes of those days included the lawyer in town who turned out to be a real live warlock! He decided to pay our little group a visit one evening, but it was only later that we became aware of his 'lower calling'. The circumstance of this was when one member of our group presented a young lady to me who had been contemplating suicide. As it turned out, she had been a part of this lawyer's coven! If this sounds like something out of a horror movie, well I guess that it was, or at least it certainly felt like it! Several of us had the honors of helping her to rescue her things out of the creepy summer house where she had been kept by her warlock master. I'll never forget some of the occult trappings that we removed and later brought to the dump to be burned: some kind of satanic manual and other occult books, crystals used in satanic rituals, and a voodoo doll! All of this paraphernalia was carted to the town dump; to make sure that it was actually destroyed, another lady and I took care of the matter of burning these things ourselves. Amazingly, the books didn't want to burn and neither did the voodoo doll. The crystals were resistant to being smashed as well. After much prayer and several unpleasant hours at the dump, the task was finally completed. Kelly, the young girl who had been ensnared by the warlock attorney, ended up staying with me for a while until she could find a job and secure an apartment. She received the Lord into her life and was so anxious to seal her newly found faith in Jesus that we had to baptize her in my bathtub! I should explain to the reader here that all of this took place in New England during the cold fall months. We did not have a baptistery available to us and Kelly, in her heart, could not wait for summer and the warm friendly lake or river waters.

Let it be stated that our adversary, the warlock, didn't take any of this lying down! He tried to put some curses on me and made some threats. But as I explained earlier, I had a childlike faith and excitement about the Lord and matters of the Spirit, and so I can honestly say that I had no fear whatsoever regarding his dark pronouncements. The enemy can only work through fear, just as the Lord only works through faith, so I guess that my undaunted lack of fear made me untouchable! As I write this account, years later, I'm a little older and a little bit wiser, so please pay attention to me when I say that I wouldn't recommend that anyone step into this kind of situation alone, or without a good sound preparation in spiritual matters of this sort! And certainly, don't go looking for such a ministry......if the Lord has called you to deal with the occult and demons in a kind of deliverance ministry, believe me, it'll find you!

I could share other stories of this sort, but I'd rather put the spotlight on our glorious God, rather than on the works of demons. It's enough to state that God has given us power over the enemy and that He wants all of us to walk in freedom and deliverance from the powers of darkness. The other statement I want to make here is that as one begins to go deeper with the Lord, recognizing His Supernatural Presence, one naturally becomes aware of the supernatural presence of Satan and his hoards of demons as well! I'm sorry to tell you this dear saint, but the realm of the spirit has both, God and His angels, and Satan and his fallen angels, better known as demons! If you don't believe this, then you haven't made it past first base in your walk with the Lord.

What else can I say about this time in the Lakelands? I saw eyesight restored and teeth receive new shiny fillings. I saw God perform many signs and wonders and how wonderful it was! But, I still had a long journey ahead of me in my pursuit of really knowing Him. It was said of Moses in Psalm 103:7 that he knew the 'ways' of the Lord, while in contrast, the children of Israel only knew His 'acts':

He made known his ways to Moses,
His acts to the children of Israel.

I still felt desperately lacking in my relationship with God. It is true that I had been given an introductory course on the 'acts' of God and 'Who He is', but I was only at the very beginning stages of knowing His 'ways'.

Looking back over my personal journey, I believe that I can make this first-hand assessment: we come to know Him, and therefore His ways, through the trials, tribulations, challenges, and seemingly insurmountable obstacles, that get thrown in front of us throughout the course of our lives. How we handle these situations will determine the kind of relationship we develop with God. If we actively invite Him to intervene and guide us through these situations, then not only will we see victory, but we will end up knowing Him better. These are the times that we naturally begin pressing in to know Him more deeply and to understand His Word. We find ourselves searching Him out and dwelling in the Word of God, the Bible, to learn more about Him and His ways so that we can apply this knowledge to our circumstances. But, if we try to resolve matters on our own, by-passing God as we haphazardly wing our way through life's journey under our own steam and understanding, then we might as well tell God that we don't need Him or want Him meddling in our affairs. This is a very dangerous condition indeed for anyone to find himself in!

And so to get back to this part of my story, little did I know what would await me following my experiences in the Lakelands. What I did know, though, was that my time spent there, complete with all of its tests, trials obstacles, and spiritual adventures, became 'part and parcel' of my supernatural education! I'm convinced that God permitted and orchestrated every single challenge and blessing that came my way. No person, group, or organization that I came into contact with was by accident. No, nothing was by accident. The Almighty, my Heavenly Father, 'Abba', created a special designer path for me to follow, one that would bring me progressively closer and closer to Him if I would only act in obedience as I sought His Face! Yes, this was only the beginning…much more would follow.

Chapter Four

"Seven Years of Preparation"

It was January of 1985 when I packed up my eleven year-old daughter and as many personal belongings as I could fit into our little yellow Chevrolet. I left the Lakelands knowing that the Lord was finished with me there. Sensing that the sheep had come to an impasse, and that it would take another kind of personality or situation to get them moving forward, I shared this with my denominational supervisor and tried to prepare the sheep. The greatest hindrance to the flock seemed to be that the men were not maturing spiritually the way they should. I was convinced that they needed a strong male pastor to lead and guide them and to serve as a role model. Such a man came our way and he was endorsed by our Pentecostal denomination. Unfortunately though, I learned later on that this brother wasn't very Pentecostal himself in that he quenched the Holy Spirit and discouraged the sheep from flowing in the gifts of the Spirit. This didn't settle well with some of the sheep and so they moved on to one Spirit-filled congregation that was nearly an hour away. I had known and respected the pastor of this ministry, and though I was sad that the work in the Lakelands had been broken up, I could also see the Lord's hand in what had occurred. In recent years, I have been able to correspond with and visit some of the sheep, and so I know that the transfer to this other sheepfold caused them to grow and really thrive. I also recognized that the Lord sent me there, the crazy 'on fire for God' woman, for the purpose of getting things stirred up and the ball rolling spiritually. In order for that to happen, He had to place me in a visible position, thus the role as 'pastor' despite my female gender! The training and education that I received from the Lord during those years in the Lakelands was not only supernatural, it was practical as well. And though I would never choose to be in such a role again, I can really appreciate the challenges and responsibilities that such a position demands. Not only that, but the strong battles that ensue as well as the enemy attempts to block the

Kingdom of God from moving forward.

So my little yellow car, packed full to overflowing with my daughter Alice and most of our worldly goods, headed south to Florida. I left having almost no clues about what was next on God's agenda for me, though some seeds had been planted a few months earlier regarding a future ministry or vision…but that was not for now. All I knew was that I needed to go to Florida and that for a few weeks there would be a place for me to stay at the guest house belonging to one church on Florida's east coast. My parents had settled way on the other side of Florida a couple of years earlier and my older sister lived nearby. My younger sister, who was attending a college in the region, was also in the vicinity, making the migration of most of my immediate family to Florida complete. Only a brother remained in New England.

I need to pause and point out here that my poor family, at this point, probably didn't quite know what to do with me. I knew that they loved me and wanted me to be happy, but somehow there was a growing feeling of separation as I launched more deeply into what they understood to be 'religion'. Now, I'd rather use the word 'relationship' with God rather than 'religion' because that's what it had all come down to for me…my relationship with Him! My approach to life since I had left to enter seminary in Boston did not always seem to be very practical I'm sure. No longer could I build my security, hopes, and aspirations on what looked like the wise thing to do based on the world's standards…but then again, I wasn't 'of the world' any longer though I lived in it. In my search for the Living God, I had slipped over to the other side where I had experienced His Kingdom and His Presence. How I longed for my family to understand this; then they would not only know Him, but they would better understand me, their 'peculiar' daughter and sibling!

And so from 1985 through 1992 there were what I'd like to refer to as seven years of preparation for what would follow…my being 'sent out' to serve God's people, first in Russia, and then later in Israel. But first came those seven years to grow on when so many important things happened. Though I will be tempted to write about all the episodes during this time, I'll restrain myself from doing so simply because it might constitute a book in itself! Generally speaking, though, let me say that this was a time of really learning to trust God on a higher level, as well as a time to expand my understanding of spiritual matters, especially regarding the prophetic. God had given me a kind of 'spiritual dad' to learn from and an opportunity to receive encouragement to develop as well in the area of 'teacher' in the Body of Christ. Just as important, it was a time to pull back a bit from the demands of tending the sheep and to give my daughter, Alice, some much needed attention. Finally, it was a time to wait on the Lord as He shaped His vision for me regarding the future.

There were many changes associated with this time period. For a starter, I lived in two different States, Florida initially, with a later move to Tennessee. Except for maybe nine months or so, I found secular employment as an English teacher and a teacher of mentally handicapped adults in Florida. But being unable to secure employment as a teacher when I moved to Tennessee, I worked as a social worker for the State in the areas of child abuse, foster care and adoptions. Then there was also another change regarding my ministerial credentials. The Pentecostal denomination that I had been affiliated with in New England seemed so different in the South that I felt to turn in my paperwork once again. Somehow, being rubber-stamped by a church organization seemed less and less important to me. There is a time and place to be set apart by the laying on of hands, I suppose. But for me, I wanted God's Hand on me and only His approval! I was beginning to realize that the true validation for any ministry comes from God and God alone.

Chapter Five

"Introduction to the Prophetic"

My first few months in Florida were both strange and wonderful. Alice and I stayed at a church guesthouse on Florida's east coast for maybe three weeks. It was so hard to settle down and pray there, though the folks who ran the house were kind and tried to be helpful. Alice didn't quite know what to do with herself and neither did I. The couple that ran the house were into health food specials, and so the menu had things like seaweed and purple cactus juice as part of the diet. Everything seemed so strange to both of us! I had never lived outside of New England and so Florida was quite a change.

A week or two after arriving in Florida, I looked up some old friends of mine from the Northeast who had migrated to the central part of Florida. They invited Alice and I to stay with them for awhile until I knew where God was going to put us. I took them up on their gracious offer. Miraculously, God had released some money to get me through these first few months; it came from the ministerial pension fund associated with the first denomination that I had held paperwork with. Like I said, it was a real miracle that they let me have it as the first time that I inquired about withdrawing the money, (based on my having left the denomination), they stated that I'd have to wait until retirement age...that was their policy! I felt the Holy Spirit telling me to inquire again. I did so feeling a bit foolish for asking a second time, but guess what, it was really God in action! A short time after I received a letter telling me that they would be glad to forward me a check as soon as the paper work could be put through. Because of this, I was not only able to make it through until God settled me somewhere, but I was able to share some of this blessing with my friends who were struggling financially. God came through once again.

While visiting with these friends, I became aware of a Gospel tent in their town that had been set up in a shopping center parking lot. Though I realized that I could walk into the middle of most anything, my curiosity outweighed my caution and caused me to check out what was going on inside. That first evening, taking Alice by the hand, we entered just as the meeting was beginning. From the start, it was obviously a charismatic gathering, and much to my relief, not bogged down with some of the old religious trappings I associated with an earlier movement. The worship was fresh and electric, so much so, that I was quickly caught up in the heavenly realm as the Presence of God became manifest. Once the worship had wound down, a man in his early middle years wearing a white Hawaiian wedding shirt proceeded to preach and share with those who had gathered. There was a pretty good crowd that first night as I recall, and the numbers seemed to increase each consecutive night that I attended. I was so caught up with what went on there that I faithfully showed up every evening for nearly two weeks.

The man in the Hawaiian wedding shirt would figure prominently into my life and become a kind of spiritual dad for me about a year or so later. In the meantime though, the Lord brought me to Florida's west coast where my family resided and planted me in a teaching job there with a local middle school, yet another miracle my Heavenly Father orchestrated! (I was offered this teaching position after speaking with the principal of the school for a total of five minutes, even before I had filled out the application. Considering that I didn't hold a current teacher's license from any state, this was an almost unheard of situation!) Now going back to my opening statement in this paragraph, about a year later I made a trip to go visit Martha and Barry, the friends that I had stayed with in central Florida. To my great surprise, the 'tent' ministry had moved into a rented building and had evolved into a rather dynamic 'church' ministry. Martha and Barry were very active leaders in this church and Martha was playing the keyboard to assist in leading worship during some of the services. They invited me to visit a service with them and so I did.

Now, what I haven't mentioned up to this point is that the man God used to establish this ministry called himself a prophet. He was also a gifted musician, worship leader, and preacher who flowed rather dynamically in the gifts of the Spirit. For the sake of this book, I'm going to call him Bro. George. Never before had I been around such a thing, this prophetic gift in action. I would listen in amazement as Bro. George would speak out things to strangers about their past or current situations and then proceed to speak words of encouragement, sometimes correction, and words that described future events. It was almost uncanny how the Lord would show him things, seemingly as if he had previously 'read all their mail' before meeting them! I had no idea that God would speak in such a way today. Up until that point, I had only understood prophecy as it related to the Old Testament prophets and more as a Word from God to a nation or a people. Actually, I guess that I hadn't thought about personal prophetic words too much except as in the case of the Lord giving someone a 'word of knowledge' about another person…this can be part of the prophetic flow, yet still different from what I was being introduced to.

During my first visit to Bro. George's church in central Florida, a close friend who had come along with me and I received a prophetic word together. Parts of this prophecy were specifically for her, while other parts were spoken to me. One portion of the prophecy had to do with a joint prophetic word that very accurately described some of the ministry things that we had been doing together in our local church, neighborhood, and at the hospital where we were both volunteers for the Chaplain's department. Remember that this man who was delivering God's word knew absolutely nothing about us, yet he was hitting directly on both of our situations…what blew me away the most was his addressing what God would be doing with me in the future. He spoke about passports and visas and a very active ministry overseas. At that point, I had only traveled once down the U.S. eastern seaboard, leaving the state of Maine to go to Florida. The only foreign country I had ever visited was Canada, traveling just a short distance over the Maine border to go into New Brunswick where my family had relatives. Yet, what this man was saying bore witness to me because it was a confirmation of the things that the Lord had started to speak to me about just before I had left the church setting in the Lakelands a couple of years earlier. As I write this, I am currently holding my third U.S. passport and have collected visa stamps from six different countries! Much of that prophetic word has not only been fulfilled, it also continues into the present. But, though this prophecy was given some time early in 1987, it wasn't until April of 1993 that the Lord launched me out to Moscow, Russia after a brief stay in a missionary training center in the South.

I quickly became very involved in Bro. George's church. Despite the long traveling distance, I was almost always present for the services because I couldn't seem to get enough of the Presence of God that I would normally experience there. I can remember one time bringing my older sister with me to visit. She was so overwhelmingly confronted with the sweet Presence of the Holy Spirit that she exclaimed out loud so that all could hear, "Jesus is here!" That was a major thing for my sister as she had such a reserved and quiet personality, especially in a church setting. But she was right. There was a strong anointing during the services. Sometimes, the Glory of the Lord was so heavy and so strong that one could barely stand in His Presence!

As I look back, I have to recognize that the Lord used the backdrop of this ministry as a real training camp for me. I got to rub elbows with many who associated themselves with the prophetic movement of that time, and in my association with them, I got to not only see the good that could be produced by the prophetic move of the Holy Spirit, but the bad as well. That bad came in the form of another spirit who liked to masquerade himself as one of God's prophets. I learned that a very subtle mixture of flesh and spirit could produce tainted and damaging results in the life of the receiver of that word. Because our words contain power, whether prompted by the Spirit of God or manipulated by the spirit of man or demon, they can take on flesh, so to speak. The important thing was to discern the origin of what was spoken…did the prophecy come from a clean and totally yielded vessel or were there some 'kinks' in the one assuming the role of prophet. I came to the conclusion that this had to be one of the most dangerous and misused of the gifts of the Holy Spirit, while at the same time it could hold the greatest blessing when it was genuinely from the Lord and under His control. As a result, I found myself longing to flow in this gift, but at the same time riding my foot on the brakes because of the 'misuse' and 'abuse' that I observed in the false prophets.

By the beginning of 1988, I was asked to take on the mid-week services at the church. Bro. George had actually set up housekeeping in a neighboring state and found it difficult to be in central Florida except for the main services on the weekends. There was yet another transition going on in his life and in the life of the ministry and so in his seeking the Lord about this matter, he felt that I was the one to fill in during the week. At the time, I was teaching full time in the public school system on the west coast and so the drive to and from the church wasn't easy. I would get out of school around 4:00 or 4:30 P.M., gather up my daughter Alice who had just finished her school day, drive through a fast food restaurant, get onto the interstate and an hour and a half later we'd pull into the church yard. (After the return trip home, we'd both flop into bed late and rise up early to greet the next school day). It wasn't the most relaxed situation for me, but somehow I'd gather my composure and the Lord would equip me to teach His Word and lead the mid-week flock in some worship. Laying aside the practical and physical demands of the situation, I was really thriving in God's anointing at this time. I gained a new confidence in handling His Word as a kind of prophetic teaching ability developed. The Lord was always faithful to give me fresh word and revelation for the current situation that the flock was facing. They received me in the position that the Lord had temporarily called me to and so I became a kind of assistant or associate of the ministry. Much transpired over the next year or so and eventually my role increased even more as Bro. George found it harder and harder to make the weekly trek to central Florida. At last, I was asked to move to the town where the church was located so that I could be more available to the ministry. I am tempted to share a lot more about my days and involvement with this ministry, but at this juncture I probably need to move on with my story... and so this brings me to the hills of Tennessee!

Chapter Six

"'Raven Food' plus Other Lessons in Faith"

When I gave my notice to the school department in Florida where I had taught, I almost couldn't believe that I was doing such a thing! It was a rather bold step to take, but I knew that the Lord was telling me to leave Florida. And so I pulled up the proverbial stakes once again, put my little home up for sale, (leaving it in the hands of a friend who happened to be a real estate agent), and made the long drive to reach my destination in the hills of Tennessee. That's where Bro. George and his wife resided, and that's where I felt the Lord was directing me to go. As I look back over those four or so years in this state, I can say that I didn't miss God in making the move, but also, I didn't end up going for the reasons that I had originally thought either! Somehow I had envisioned a ministry being planted in Tennessee and my needing to be there to assist Bro. George. Eventually, one did emerge ever so briefly and it served God's purposes for a season, but basically, Bro. George had understandingly become disheartened with the difficulties of tending the sheep, and so focusing on a different kind of 'planting' at this time, he invested himself heavily in his fruit farm and jam business. I understood why he felt that he needed a reprieve from the ministry things because I knew a lot about what he had been through. Yes, the berry bushes didn't jab you with their thorns unexpectedly or talk negative things behind your back! The hard manual labor and the 'ups and downs' of running a business were preferable to the negative antics of the sheep. But, because of this season of his withdrawal from active ministry, I felt that I had lost some of the spiritual covering that I so desperately needed during this time of my geographical and 'spiritual' relocation.

My first five months in Tennessee were challenging to say the least. I quickly located a nice little mobile home to rent that was situated on a grassy private lot, but finding a job was yet another matter. I was most diligent in my job search, spreading about one hundred resumes within a fifty to seventy-five mile radius of my home. I had filled out so many employment applications that I kept the BIC pen company in business! But still there was no job in sight, despite the fact that I held two degrees and had a very good work history. Even the part time deli job didn't come through for me, notwithstanding the numerous teaching and professional positions that I qualified for.

One day, a couple of months into my desperate search, I slowed down long enough to finally seek the Lord about this problem. This, of course, was something I should have done right at the very start. But 'yours truly' was still trying to maintain a certain amount of control over the matters of everyday life, while at the same time, working within the framework of the bigger faith step, i.e. the physical move. My spirit was so cluttered with the static of cares, worry and frustration that I don't know how the Lord ever managed to get me to hear Him, but He did and 'loud and clear' at that! I'll never forget what He said, "I'm going to feed you like I did the prophet Elijah." That was it...one brief but powerful word from God! I shuddered for a moment as I reacted to what had been spoken. I seemed to recall something about Elijah's hanging out around a brook and the ravens coming by to make periodic food drops. I grabbed my Bible and quickly leafed through the two books of Kings. There it was in I Kings 17:1-6:

And Elijah the Tishbite, of the inhabitants of Gilead, said to Ahab, "As the Lord God of Israel lives, before whom I stand, there shall not be dew nor rain these years, except at my word." Then the word of the Lord came to him, saying, "Get away from here and turn eastward, and hide by the brook Cherith, which flows into the Jordan. And it will be that you shall drink from the brook, and I have commanded the ravens to feed you there." So he went and did according to the word of the Lord, for he went and stayed by the Brook Cherith, which flows into the Jordan. The ravens brought

42

him bread and meat in the morning, and he drank from the brook.

My first BIG LESSON in faith had begun! And yes, miracle of miracles, the Lord truly sent me food via the ravens. Where did it come from? I don't exactly know…some came from here and some came from there. In the end, I managed to get through five months with almost all of my bills paid on time. Once near the end of this dry time, I had to borrow some money from my parents for a car payment, but I was able to pay that back the following month because the Lord had at last supplied me with a job. As I look back at this time, I marvel at God's faithfulness and I can understand now why He put me through this 'dry' season when the proverbial natural rains had been shut up, but not the rain from heaven. It was because I would not only need this early faith lesson in the faraway places that He would later send me, but there would be other advanced lessons in faith in the future as well.

The dryness resulting from joblessness had been remedied but another kind of dryness continued for most of my time spent in Tennessee. Though I found myself stationed in the heart of the 'Bible Belt' (or so they call it), my search for a church home, one that was alive with the Spirit of God, was every bit as fruitless as my initial job searches. I visited a number of churches in my own town and in neighboring towns, but there always seemed to be something missing or something out of order. I wasn't looking for a perfect church, just a 'real' church. After visiting about a dozen congregations I gave up. Like I mentioned earlier, Bro. George did eventually start a small congregation about a year and a half before I left Tennessee to go to a missionary training school and this did provide me with some spiritual underpinning. But, it was nothing in comparison to the move of God that I had been in the middle of while living in Florida. For the first two and a half years or so of my Tennessee adventure, it was a spiritual dry desert. In this desert of isolation from spiritual brothers and sisters, I never purposefully moved away from the Lord, but I recognized that I was becoming dry myself and without the kind of hope and excitement that I once carried. Bro. George and his wife were dealing with their own things and so I felt partially detached from them as well. Still, I kept pressing on and eventually emerged from my dry desert. But before that happened, I hit a kind of crisis point after a couple of years and got it into my head that I needed to go back to Florida. There, at least, I had some family and perhaps I could get back into the school system that I had left.

I'll never forget Bro. George's words when I told him that I wanted to go back to Florida; he said that it was like going back to Egypt! About this matter he was correct, but I knew my own condition…I felt alone and let down by almost everyone and in some ways wondered where my God was in the middle of all this. Herein was yet another opportunity for a different kind of lesson in faith. Without getting a clear word from the Lord regarding all of this, I pushed ahead in the flesh, making several trips to Florida to scope out teaching positions. I was so certain that the Lord was going to return me there that I began packing boxes and stacking them in the corners of my living room. It's comical to me now as I think back, but it wasn't so funny back then as I tried to take charge once again of my own life. My error in all of this was to speak faith into the changes that my flesh wanted rather than to exercise faith based on what God wanted. And do you know what? The Lord blocked me every inch of the way and, looking back, I'm so thankful that He did! Like the worn rubber on my car tires from all the wasted trips to Florida, I was permitted by the One in control to wear myself down. The Lord even permitted me to come within a hair's breadth of being offered a teaching position. Shortly after arriving back in Tennessee after my final 'job' trek to Florida, I received a phone call from the principal of one school. She called me to let me know that the teacher I was slated to replace had changed her mind at the last minute and wanted to come back for the upcoming school year. I groaned as I looked at all of those boxes that I had so diligently packed! Like it or not, for reasons unknown to me at the time, the Lord had grounded me in Tennessee. And so I unpacked the contents of the boxes and continued on with my Social Counselor position with the State doing my best to immerse myself in my work. In assisting my young clients, children who were victims of abuse, I had hoped to at least find some degree of satisfaction from serving them, while at the same time I was in the process of trying to figure out what God's intentions were for me.

By the end of 1991, Bro. George had started a little congregation. Emerging from a Bible study that he had conducted in his home, it never really multiplied much in number but God had a plan and a purpose, at least for a season, for this particular flock. As I am ever learning, *"All things work together for good"*, as Paul writes in Romans 8:28. And so some of that 'good' purpose may have been not only to benefit Bro. George, who was starting to re-involve himself with sheep, but also to assist this little sheep as well who needed the Lord to restore her vision regarding future things, things that had been spoken about just prior to leaving New England.

Having said all this, my desert experience in Tennessee was coming to a close. The Lord was refreshing me and restoring my vision. Why I had to go through such a time, I'll never know exactly, but as I have explained, there were important lessons about faith and trust that needed to be learned. Not only that, but in my isolation I was also reminded that God alone was the One to be sought after in times of trouble. Man is frail flesh and imperfect; only the God inside of him can rise to the occasion of victory over the day's troubles. It was in the desert, in the wilderness, that the children of Israel were tested. It was there that their weaknesses and imperfect natures were exposed. But it was also there that the Lord showed some of His greatest miracles. Yes, God was faithful to bring them out to the other side; He didn't just leave them there, though they first had to wander for forty years…I had wandered for nearly four. Now I was coming out to the other side. I could feel it. Another transition was about to take place.

Chapter Seven

"The Vision Begins to Take on Flesh"

During the summer of 1992, Brother George and his wife decided to attend a missionary conference in a neighboring southern state. They took along several of the sheep from our little flock; I just happened to be one of them. Actually, I had no great preliminary stirring to attend this particular conference nor did I have any great expectations for its outcome. I left Tennessee only with an average curiosity to see what it would be all about, but as the conference wound down, I knew that what had taken place there had somehow connected with the vision God had given me more than seven years earlier just before leaving the Lakelands. It's hard to describe exactly what was taking place inside of me as I listened to each successive missionary speak. All I can say is that my heart was ready to burst wide open with excitement and strong emotions that were beyond a natural response or reaction to what was being shared. I was somehow caught up in another dimension that separated me from the everyday realm. All that I could do was to sit there 'alone' among the crowd of participants in a packed auditorium as each word spoken by the missionaries would be driven ever more deeply into my heart, propelled as it were by the Spirit of God who spoke through these vessels.

At the end of the conference, as we pulled out of the complex that housed the church and missionary training school that I would later attend, my thoughts wandered back to the end of 1984. Just before heading for Florida I had come across Steve Lightle's book, Exodus II. I was not only impacted by this man's testimony describing how God had trained him to hear His Voice and to walk in obedience, but for the first time I really locked into the prophecies in the Old Testament regarding the Second Exodus. I consumed each page of the book with ravenous hunger as the author described the supernatural unfolding of events regarding the modern day return of the Jews from the nations to their Divinely appointed Homeland, Israel. The author shared about how God had spoken to various individuals and groups, mostly within Europe, about making preparations to assist the Jews who would be coming out of the 'North', the countries of the old U.S.S.R., in order to make their way into Israel. The whole book stirred me so much that by the end of my reading it I had a strong impression that one day I too would have something to do with this Second Exodus!

At this point of my story I need to weave another important thread into this tapestry of my vision, otherwise the description would be incomplete. It has to do with my unusual drawing to Israel and the Jewish people that began years ago. I can recall, as if it were yesterday, telling my father on a number of occasions that I had to go to Israel. Not knowing if my yearning for Israel was a brief visit or permanent stay, something deep inside of me was attracting me there. When I would talk about Israel, my father was more than puzzled about this, I'm sure. But he always good-naturedly shrugged it off as just one more element of strange behavior exhibited by his middle daughter who, "got mixed up with the babies in the nursery", as my mother used to tell me. My pronouncements about Israel date back to my teens and twenties. They were accompanied by yet another kind of intrigue that was directly related; I can only describe this intrigue as being more than just a mere curiosity about Judaism.

The reader needs to understand here that I grew up in a small city in Maine, (actually more the size of a large town), that was at least ninety percent French Roman Catholic. Most of the people who populated this area of Maine had relatives who had migrated from Quebec, Canada. In fact, if you resided in this town and your last name was French, it was almost certain that you not only spoke French, but that you were Roman Catholic as well. My family name was indeed French but in these two identifying factors I was the exception. Dad's parents had gotten angry with their local Catholic priest during the depression years in America when he pressed them for offering money they didn't have. As a result, they swore off church and this attitude got passed on to my father and many of his siblings. My French-speaking grandparents also thought that it was more American to rear their children with only English being spoken at home. So the French part of my heritage somehow got lost as well. Back to the other ten percent of my hometown, it can best be described as representing the mainline Protestant denominations plus one small Jewish synagogue. So as you can see, this was not an area that hosted a large Jewish community, nor was Judaism a religion that was well understood by the folks I grew up with.

There were two Jewish girls in my class at school. They never said much about what they believed, but we all knew that they were different. Don't get me wrong, Sandy and Dina were very much accepted by their classmates and a part of the school scene, yet at the same time there was something unseen that separated them from the rest of us. I keenly sensed this unseen element and wanted to ask them a lot of questions yet held myself back feeling that it would be impolite to do so. I can remember one birthday party I attended that their parents allowed them to go to. Before the girls arrived, my friend's mother, (the friend who was having the birthday party), cued the rest of us in that Sandy and Dina would not be able to eat the ham sandwiches that had been prepared. And so I learned that Jewish people don't eat pork, but it wasn't until years later that I began to understand much more about what being Jewish really meant.

Returning to my experience at the missionary conference, I can tell you that a decision was made during the long ride home to begin to move out in faith with what the Lord had been telling me. The vision had to start to take on flesh if it was ever going to move forward. This was clearly God's timing for the process to begin and I knew it! As I discussed what was going on inside of me with Bro. George, he seemed to sense this as well, and so there was some much needed encouragement and confirmation offered. I arrived home and greeted my daughter Alice that night knowing that I was destined to go overseas one day soon and that my target population had to do with Russian Jews and Israel. Alice, who was eighteen when all of this transpired, would soon be completing her senior year in high school. She had plans to enter the army after graduation so that she could later benefit from the G.I. Bill that would cover her college expenses. And so as it turned out, we both left home at the same time! Alice left home to enter her training at army boot camp, while her mother entered another kind of boot camp. It was the missionary training school that had hosted the missionary conference I attended earlier. The next three or four months would prove to be extremely challenging for both of us.

Chapter Eight

"FMC & A Most Unusual Dream"

After the first month or so at Faith Missionary Center, I had started to question God's purposes for sending me there before launching me out to my assigned harvest field. For this particular session there were only a handful of students, and the maturity level of the student body varied greatly. I got along fine with everyone, but there was really only one couple that I could relate to besides a girl named Wanita from Mexico. My young Mexican friend, mature beyond her natural years, had a serious walk with the Lord. For some reason she became drawn to me, so I in turn, a kind of big sister, felt to take her under my wing. Communication, though, was a real challenge as she knew no English and I could barely muster up a few words from my Spanish that dated back to a college course in the 70's! Despite that, I felt much closer to her than most of the American students with the exception of that one couple.

As with most missionary training schools, the goal of Faith Missionary Center was to prepare its students for the challenges of living in a different culture by teaching them how to be an effective tool for the promotion of the Kingdom of God. The ability to relate to both the nationals and other missionaries that the prospective missionary would serve and labor among was the main focus. And, central to this focus was the idea that the students needed to learn about walking in humility and obedience. This kind of training philosophy seemed to flow down from the school's director and founder, Bro. Willie, a man in his 70's who was best known among the brethren for his undaunted faith and humble character. He was a marvelous example for all of us, staff and students alike, of a man who had responded obediently to the Lord's call to go out to the nations to preach the Gospel. What was so amazing about all this was that Bro. Willie wouldn't have a penny in his pocket, yet the Lord always supplied what was needed for the almost endless "Go Ye" missions that he was sent out on. And so by his life, this man provided a real example of one who prospered from his faith, unhindered as he was by the natural realm of finances that are normally needed to carry out the work of the ministry. But the school's focus on shaping humility in the students was yet another matter. I could see what they were trying to accomplish with their 'pride busting' regimen. I could even understand why such training was necessary, especially after I had spent some time with the brethren on the Russian mission field. Yet as I compliantly submitted to this particular molding program, I wondered how the Lord defined humility and how that stacked up to the philosophy and methods of the Faith Missionary Center staff?

So, for better or for worse, I good-naturedly went along with the program. It didn't bother me to be the last in line at mealtime and I enjoyed cleaning the toilets because I could be alone with the Lord while tending to this task. I cooked, cleaned, washed, and served the food, weeded the gardens and raked the leaves. These were all familiar tasks that I had never considered beneath me. I went around like 'plain Jane' as the women were not permitted to wear any make-up or jewelry. My daily attire consisted of very unstylish long skirts and dresses to work in because the women were not allowed to wear pants except during exercise time when everyone, without exception, had to participate. In addition to all of these rules and restrictions, the students were allowed to go into town only once a week on Saturday mornings. Though I sometimes felt a bit like a child rather than an adult in all of this, I was obedient and took it all in stride with a good attitude. I do believe that I passed the humility test in this regard.

One thing that I was most thankful for was having my own room so that I could pray and study unhindered. Normally, two students would have been put together as the two beds in my room indicated, but our class was small and that meant that there would be a little more room to spread out. The main pieces of furniture in my room, other than a wooden chair and dresser for my clothes, were two antique hospital beds that had been donated to the school. Maybe you've been unfortunate enough to spend several nights on such a piece of furniture in a hospital setting. The bed had a really stiff plastic coated mattress and the head of the bed was raised or lowered using an old hand crank. Because the frame of the bed was quite high off the floor, I had to learn to pole vault myself up into it. I must say that even my lumpy, bumpy, homemade mattress that was constructed of sewed together blankets and old quilts, the one that I later slept on in Russia, was a bastion of comfort compared to this missionary training bed!

I would ask the reader to please be patient with me here because I'm not really complaining about all the above, I'm just trying to paint a kind of a picture for you. As a matter of fact, as I look back, I have to chuckle a little bit at some of the funny circumstances of my special training! What did present a problem for me though was that the students were extremely limited regarding communication with friends and loved ones. We were only allowed to receive phone calls something like once or twice a week. Under normal circumstances this would not have been troubling, but during my stay at FMC this rule especially impacted me because my daughter was having a very difficult time with her army training. I felt that it was important, as her mother, to be more available to her. In fact, she ended up having stress fractures on both her ankles from the running and exercising that was quite rigorous, and eventually she ended up being discharged from the army. When this happened, Alice went to stay with my older sister Regina. She not only left the army extremely discouraged about the turn of events, but she left somewhat hardened by the negative army environment that she had been in. As I became aware of the situation, I came very close to pulling out of my own 'boot camp' so that I could try to salvage my daughter. As difficult as it was, though, the Lord caused me to hold on a just a bit longer and so I did. Now I can understand why, but back then it was only obedience that caused me to stay on. This may have been one of the first situations where I was truly forced to thrust myself into deep intensive prayer in the form of spiritual warfare. Praying this way meant survival as the enemy applied increasing pressure on me to leave FMC. Though I felt great concern for my daughter and didn't want to place any further burdens on my older sister, I recognized that this was one of those 'sacrificing Isaac' times for me when the Lord required me to put Him above all else, including my daughter Alice. My mother's heart struggled intensely with this one. But now I realize that had I left when I wanted to, that the connection with Russia may never have happened and all the other things that followed as well. And so now I see why the enemy gave me such a hard time. This all happened in November of '92 and my missionary training wasn't scheduled to wind down until the end of May or June of '93. But the Lord knew the real schedule, His schedule, and praise God as it turned out the Faith Missionary Center class of '93 graduated in December of '92 instead! Because of the small group of students and financial considerations, I think, this decision was made much to my personal relief. As my missionary preparation time came to a close, the Lord gave me about three and a half months to settle Alice before He launched me out to Russia.

But before leaving this chapter of my life, I must tell the reader about my last week at FMC. This was my breakthrough 'week' that the enemy never wanted me to arrive at! He knew that once the ball got rolling with God's vision for me that it would be very difficult to stop the momentum. Anyway, this is what happened:

It was almost graduation time when the staff decided to show the students one last mission's film. I had seen a number of these films over the past few months. There was the mission field documentary about China, and India, and some country in Africa...the list goes on. Each time that I had watched one of these films, I would become frustrated because I felt that I was wasting precious time where I sat. The truth was that I wanted to be on the field doing something for the Lord, not just watching it be done by others. Going hand in hand with this desire to 'go' and 'do', the contents of these films would stir up my emotions for the lost sheep of whatever country I was viewing at the time. This would, in turn, cause great emotional havoc inside of me for the next few days following. It wasn't just me, I learned, who went on these emotional roller coaster rides during these films, but the one couple that I had spoken about earlier. They too were ready to go out and 'do'!

So when this last film of my academic year came around just prior to graduation time, I determined to sit there and watch it with an invisible protective wall, a wall that would be placed between me and what would appear on the screen. I calmly sat there void of emotion as the subject title flashed across the screen. Noting that the nation represented in this film was Russia, with each successive flick of footage I became more determined than ever to fight any luring reaction to what was being shown. But then it happened…it was as if one particular frame or scene had become frozen in time. I watched in amazement as simple Russian country folk, clad in their typical native dress, filled the screen. These men and women were not representative of their more metropolitan brothers and sisters who dwelt in Moscow or St. Petersburg. But in my dream, they symbolized the citizens of Mother Russia. My thoughts flashed back to an unusually detailed, four-part dream that I had had about a month before entering FMC. One part of the dream depicted the very people that I was looking at! I had never connected the men and women of my dream with Russia, but there they were before my eyes as big as life! There was no mistake about all this as the Holy Spirit bore witness to my unfolding revelation. On the contrary, it was His revelation and this was the moment in time that He had chosen to disclose it!

The film ended but not the vision. For a while, I too sat frozen in time like that key segment of film footage. I needed to understand what was happening to me. Just months before, I had entered FMC believing that God would be sending me out to Israel. Was it possible that I had missed God so badly on this point? During our community prayer times at the missionary school, I would always go over to the large wall-sized map and put my finger on Israel. "This is the place that God is sending me", I would proudly proclaim only to hear Bro. Willie's reply that it wasn't time for Israel yet! I think that he made this proclamation more in the sense of the harvest field, the chosen people of God, not being ripe for the picking yet, though he may have also been prophetic in his pronouncement regarding me personally. Yes, I would work with the Russian Jews, but somehow I had always envisioned that being in Israel! Now there seemed to be a new element introduced into the vision. Could it be that God was really sending me to Russia first? I reviewed that part of my dream that I had connected with the film. In it I saw a number of men and women who had gathered in an open market place. Indeed, as I now understood it, these were Russian men and women! I waited with them as they got onto a bus that would carry them to an airport. As the first bus load of these people departed, I knew that it was critical to get them out first, though I myself desired to go with them. Incredibly, in this dream I had knowledge that these precious people were missionaries! Yes, missionaries! But it was only now clear to me where they were going. The Holy Spirit washed over me with revelation and understanding that only He can give. They were bound for Israel...Russian Jews bound for Israel and they were either already believers in Jesus, the one they called 'Yeshua', or because of a special openness to the Gospel set against the backdrop of 70 years of Communist rule, they would become believers! As the Lord God of Israel integrated these immigrants into their Promised Land, He would use them to ignite His fire of revival among their siblings, the sons and daughters of Jacob. But like in the dream, I would have to wait for a second bus. In my heart I paused to say, "Yes", to God regarding all of this! I was willing to go to this strange land. It was all so sudden, I acknowledged, but I had no doubt that the Lord was sending me out to Russia. One day I would get on that second bus bound for Israel. But first, as I would later learn, what was destined to transpire in Russia would be used to lay the ground work for Abba's future plans for me in Israel.

The day before leaving FMC, I sat down with Bro. Willie and the young man who would later take up his mantle as the school's director. They both listened intently as I relayed my story about the film, the dream, and Russia. Unbeknownst to me, they had close connections with one organization that desperately needed volunteers in several Russian and Ukrainian cities where they were establishing churches. Leaving FMC the following day, I went back to Tennessee anxiously waiting to be contacted by Pastor Mills, the president of this organization. It was the end of December. The following April I would be sitting on a plane bound for Moscow.

PART II

Russia, A 'Spiritual' Travelogue

Chapter Nine

"Welcome To Russia!"

There I sat, alone, on one of the narrow twin beds in my hotel room somewhere in Russia's capital city of Moscow. My attention became focused on a loudspeaker announcement that abruptly pierced my silence…what could it be, I thought? Knowing only a handful of words in Russian, I could only guess what was being said. I thought to myself, maybe it's a fire drill. But as I cautiously poked my head outside the door, I noted that no one seemed to be stirring in the hallway. I looked across to the other side of the hall. The door was open to the floor attendant's quarters. Actually, this woman was more like a dorm mother, an appointed overseer for all that transpired on her floor. In her room stood a lovely large samovar filled with hot water, while along side of it sat a friendly teapot containing a thick, black liquid that would be poured out and thinned in the guest's teacup. I was relieved that my hostess, unlike the female guards at Sherevmetreva International Airport, at least attempted a little smile and tried to communicate with me. I was most thankful for this small token of human warmth. I closed the door behind me. Safely back inside what would be my living quarters for the next three or four days, I noted that this was not like any hotel room that I had ever experienced before. In fact, nothing to this point was like anything I had ever experienced before! Yet, I remained calm and even joyfully expectant about what would lie ahead. Yes, I had made it through the dark and unfriendly international airport in Moscow where the guards acted rough and hardened and almost no one spoke English. But the Lord had given me such a supernatural peace about all this that my joy and excitement about being in Russia for God's purposes far outweighed any fear that would have been natural in my situation.

My hotel room soon gave way to a small one-bedroom apartment at the end of the metro 'blue line' in Moscow. It was a delightful little apartment, totally furnished by the elderly lady who had lived there but rented it out to me in exchange for American cash for her and her family. She probably moved in with a son or daughter while I occupied her little nest. I paid her $100 a month, which was a real windfall for her at this time. You see, the Russian economy was still in the early stages of adjusting to the changes made during 'peristroika', after the Berlin wall had come down, and the Russian ruble was very unstable. So, dollars were very much sought after as a secure source of currency.

Because I was renting out this lady's personal space, I had to be willing to live alongside not only her furnishings, but also with many of her personal belongings as well. Such things as old shoes and articles of clothing, piles of papers and books, various knick-knacks and keepsakes, and even empty glass and metal containers were stored here and there in every conceivable space. The decor was absolutely Russian! By American standards, nothing matched, but by Russian standards the various colors, designs, and patterns in the rugs and wall paper somehow strangely fit together with the other furnishings, creating a kind of cozy Russian "gingerbread house" for its American occupant. There was a small gas stove and refrigerator, but no clothes washer. Herein was the beginning of my experience with hand washing all of my clothing, something I ended up doing throughout all of my time in Russia, and as circumstances have had it, later on in Israel where I now sit writing this book. But I must be careful not to get ahead of myself here…

About twenty or twenty-five minutes from my apartment by metro was the church office for the "Christian Gospel Fellowship". CGF had been responsible for the newly planted Moscow church that I would be volunteering in. This work was no more than a year old by the time I arrived on the scene. A little background on CGF might be helpful at this juncture. This was the association of independent charismatic churches in America, presided over by Pastor Mills, who had placed me there in Russia.

CGF had started up a number of churches in various locations throughout Russia and the Ukraine. Like many other church groups and organizations from America and Europe, they would come in for a few days or weeks, present the Gospel during evangelistic crusades, and then establish churches on the foundation of new believers reaped during the harvest of the campaign. Some of these works managed to survive and even thrive while others, for whatever reasons, would boast a glorious beginning but later go into decline. In the end, though, the Seed of the Word of God was sown throughout Russia and the Ukraine, and despite man's imperfections, the Word stood and took root.

In some ways, I praise God that I was not told beforehand about the delicate situation I was about to enter, though I may have been better prepared to deal with it had someone briefed me ahead of time. Here I speak about the Moscow CFG church, its appointed missionaries, and the lack of clear direction flowing out of CFG headquarters in America. I walked into this setting looking through spiritual 'rose-colored' glasses at first, seeing everything from the perspective of excitement about what the Lord was doing in the midst of His precious Russian sheep. All too soon, though, it became apparent to me that something was very wrong and that the underlying problem had nothing at all to do with the sheep. I believe that each one of my co-laborers was well intentioned in his heart about being there in Moscow and indeed some were truly called to be there. But honestly, it felt like the enemy had managed to stir up every existing individual and collective character flaw and weakness among the missionaries, making the resulting power struggles that ensued unlike anything I had ever experienced in my life! Even the strong resistance that I had come up against in the Lakelands couldn't begin to rival this. Still, in the midst of it all, God was Sovereign and His Kingdom work went forward despite the imperfect nature of man.

I look at my time spent in Moscow and two nearby cities as God's training ground for me as I got acclimated to Russia. It was important for me to understand their values and their culture and to be able to interpret patterns of behavior and thinking that might be different from my own. In other words, I needed to know the Russian heart so that I could identify with the people God sent me to serve. And then there was the language problem. One couldn't always depend on having an interpreter around and so I quickly learned a little Russian, understanding that just a few words spoken in broken and imperfect Russian would endear the heart of the native speaker to this foreigner. Most of my Russian brothers and sisters in the church were thrilled that I was attempting to speak to them in their own tongue, no matter how imperfect my speech was, and so they exhibited great patience with me in my efforts to communicate. The only ones who did not encourage me on in my Russian were the handful of young people who were determined to practice their English with me.

My closest missionary friend in Moscow was a single lady about my age named Hanna. She showed me the ropes the first few days that I was there so that I could manage to get around on my own. I was introduced to the complex, but beautiful subway system in Moscow as well as the busses, trolley cars, and tram vies, (a kind of cable car). I learned where the open market was located and how to go about purchasing food and other items in the government stores. None of this was an easy task, especially in the government stores. The process of buying a loaf of bread, for example, meant that you first waited in a long line to get inside the store, and once inside, you had to maneuver your way to the counter where the various kinds of bread were kept. Once you got there, you usually had to persistently poke your head through the crowds of buyers who were obstructing the view of available bread and prices. When you finally were able to see what kind of bread was available that day, then the next step was to get in a line to pay the cassa, (cashier). She would tally up your order on an old wooden abacus, (there were no modern cash registers at this time in Russia), and give you a purchase ticket so that you could make a return trip to the bread counter to present your ticket to the clerk. It could easily take an hour or so just to buy one item! And then if you wanted to buy cheese, for example, you had to start the whole process again at the dairy counter. I didn't master all of this at first, especially with no knowledge of the language, but I was able to get by with fingers, hand signals and smiles as long as I was fortunate enough to be received by a good-natured and patient cassa.

This perhaps gives you some idea of the strange but wonderful environment I had to operate in. I was adventuresome and the Lord had given me an unusual love for the Russian people, and so I fared quite well under the circumstances. As time went on, and the turmoil within the missionary camp mounted, I found myself spending more and more time with the Russians and pulling away from my American counterparts. I didn't really have anything against them, but I couldn't handle the animosity that had surfaced.

While I was in Moscow, there were well-intentioned attempts at evangelism. For example, we would get on the metro and walk from car to car, distributing little Gospel tracts to the passengers. The address and time of our church meetings was stamped on the back of each tract in hopes that the reader would be interested enough to come pay us a visit. The metro passengers almost always seemed anxious to receive these little booklets and would immediately begin to read them. In fact, if someone became overlooked while the booklets were being distributed, they would usually come to us to ask for one. The Russian people, who were serious students and avid readers, were very open at this time to receive ideas from the outside world that had been so tightly closed to them for over seventy years of Communism. For this reason, the method of passing out tracts worked for awhile in Russia. What was unfortunate, though, was that if any questions arose after reading the material, neither I, nor my colleagues, had the ability to answer them or to explain the Gospel in Russian. Imperfect as the method was, some were drawn to the church because of the tracts, and there they could at least hear about Jesus with the help of a translator.

The church in Moscow met in a rented public building at one of the major subway stops, but the church office itself operated from a private rented apartment. I don't know what the current rules are right now regarding buying property in Russia and erecting buildings, but back then such a thing was not allowed. So, the many new churches that were springing up, (and there were almost too many in Moscow by this time when one considered that so much of Russia hadn't yet heard the Gospel), would rent out space in theaters, cultural centers, and hotel meeting rooms. The weekly meeting at the CGF Church was held on Sunday mornings. The main thrust of the meeting was evangelistic of course, but during this time there was also a well-run Sunday School for the children. Personally, I felt that there was more 'life' flowing in the children's program than there was in the adult congregation that seemed to be slowly heading for a decline at the point I entered this ministry. This deterioration may have had something to do with the frequent changes in staff, including the several pastors that came and went during the church's brief history. Other extensions of the church included a couple of home cell groups and what became my appointed focus, the 'English' classes! On this last item, let the reader permit me to offer explanation...

This idea of promoting the Gospel and the CGF Church via free English classes was not my idea at all. It all originated in the thoughts of the newly appointed pastor, Dan Custer, who wanted to increase the size of the dwindling sheepfold. And though everything inside of me was protesting involvement in this kind of task, I smiled and went along with it, only later realizing that the Holy Spirit truly had a purpose and a place for such a tool. Now, you've got to understand that the last thing in my mind at this time was teaching English to Russians; this was not my concept of what a missionary did! In my narrow thinking, he or she was there to preach, teach, evangelize and give instruction in the Word of God. That was it! I had no problem taking to the streets with tracts or singing Christian praise and worship songs on the street corners or in the subway entrances in order to promote the things of the Kingdom, hoping that some would receive 'Esus' ('Jesus' in Russian) as their Lord. I didn't even mind keeping the church financial books for a season, but this thing of the English classes was another matter.

As I recall, the classes were held two or three times a week. They were open to the public and so we drew people from both our church and from other churches in Moscow. We also had some students as well who didn't know the Lord and were not involved in any church at all. Though I had never taught English as a second language, I managed to invent some lesson plans and methods of my own that were based on the contents of the Bible. There was no problem attracting students as almost everyone, it seemed, wanted to learn 'American' English. Before 'peristroika', the English that had been taught in the schools and universities was 'British' English. But because of the popularity of America during this time, our Russian friends all wanted to speak English with an 'American' accent.

I can recall one class that definitely got off-track as far as English instruction was concerned, but was positively right on-track with what the Holy Spirit wanted to accomplish! During this particular class, we had been singing some simple praise and worship songs in English when the Holy Spirit just started to fall. The next thing I knew, I found myself praying for some of the students who wanted to be filled with God's Precious Spirit...and they were. The words that issued out of their mouths resembled neither English nor Russian, but rather displayed a most marvelous new language that was spoken with a 'Heavenly' accent!

Six years later in 1999, I had an occasion to be in a totally different part of Russia for purposes relating to 'aliyah' (the return of the Jews to Israel). One young couple came up to me during a mid-week church gathering and asked me if I remembered them. There was something very familiar about their faces, but I honestly wasn't able to place them. The wife had apparently been invited to visit this particular congregation in Southern Russia to share her testimony about how God had incredibly prospered them in their cosmetic business because she had promised to give the bulk of her profits to aide Jewish ministry and 'aliyah'. As her miraculous story went, she started with almost nothing, but each time she would give away most of the resulting profit, a bigger and bigger increase would result. She had taken the Word of God at face value when it spoke about sowing into the Kingdom. But even more incredibly, she had gotten hold of the Scripture in Genesis 12: 3 where God promises Abram and his seed,

> *"I will bless those who bless you,*
> *And I will curse him who curses you;*
> *And in you all the families of the earth shall be blessed."*

She had recognized the special blessing that is attached to blessing God's chosen people! And then came the punch line that thrilled my soul...this couple had attended my English classes as brand new believers! It was during this time that the Lord had gotten hold of them and the business started. I never understood exactly how the 'goings on' of the English classes had impacted them for the blessing that followed because we communicated in broken English and Russian. But somehow the Holy Spirit had used this as one of His many tools to make a Kingdom connection with his plans for this special couple. Wow! God is so good. If I had ever wondered if these English classes were productive or not, my answer was to be found in this Divinely orchestrated meeting. The Lord wanted to encourage me by permitting me to see some of His hidden fruit.

Let me pause here for just a moment to encourage those among my readers who are 'listening in' to this story and questioning what kind of fruit, if any, might be borne from some ministry or activity that the Lord has engaged you in. You may not be seeing some of the hidden fruit right now, but it doesn't mean that it's not there! I can remember picking assorted wild berries as a young girl. Some of the juiciest and plumpest fruit would be tucked away, out of sight, way under the leaves and vines. You had to work extra hard to find it, sometimes being scratched and jabbed by prickly vines and bushes as you reached into the thickets in an effort to harvest the sweetest, plumpest berries. Oh, but as you popped that luscious piece of fruit into your mouth it was worth it! And so sometimes we don't always see it at first, but I do believe that the Lord has a purpose and a plan for everything that, "those who love Him", and, "are called according to His purpose", are engaged in. As Paul explains in Romans 8:28,

And we know that all things work together for good to those who love God, to those who are called according to His purpose.

Another error that we too often make is to expect one kind of fruit, (or a particular result), from our labor when the Lord may have a very different kind of purpose in mind for what He has asked us to do. Perhaps the biggest problem in all of this, though, is the problem with our lack of patience. The fruit isn't ripe yet, but because of our impatience we pluck it from the vine prematurely. Having interrupted the ripening process, we end up eating sour fruit. Ugh! We give up before God has had a chance to bring the whole process to completion according to His time schedule... not ours!

Yes, ALL THINGS work together for good, even the unexpected romance that became a temporary heartache and distraction for me. Yet the Lord used even this situation to help move me on to Southern Russia in the late spring of 1994. This was to be the place where the 'aliyah' outreach would be birthed. But for now, I'm getting a little bit ahead of myself again, and so to continue...

Chapter Ten

"Left Behind & Other Stories"

I have so many stories to tell and so much to reflect on that I could easily fill one volume alone with what had happened to me in the Moscow area during my first year in Russia. After that, the Lord sent me many hundreds of miles away to a city in Southern Russia. The following sixteen months that I spent there would probably merit another two volumes. But alas, for the purposes of this particular book it's best to simply highlight some of these events for the reader and especially those events that demonstrate God's leading. These are some of the humorous and exciting, as well as sad and serious moments that I had the privilege to not only experience, but also to grow on!

One of my assigned tasks while being in Moscow was to accompany some of the 'short term' missionaries, as we called them, when they went out to various cities throughout Russia. These were the men who were the pastors and leaders from the congregations that belonged to the CGF, (The Christian Gospel Fellowship), who wanted to visit and bless their Russian brothers and sisters by praying with them, preaching, and encouraging them in assorted ways. Now let the reader understand that my 'missionary guide' services were not always welcomed as it meant that my expenses to travel with them had to be covered by the visiting CGF members. Yes, orders had come down from the top that no short term CGF missionaries would be allowed go out alone. Instead, they had to be accompanied by one of the 'seasoned' Moscow staff...for some reason I was chosen to do this. With 'tongue in cheek' let me say that all of my six or eight months in Russia at that point made me perhaps a little bit of an expert compared to my green counterparts. Actually by this time, I was starting to pick up some of the language and could get around fairly well. And not only that, but God had given me a special affinity with the Russian soul. This covering of Divine favor somehow nearly always made it easier to move among them.

I think that I made from four to six of these trips for the CGF. It truly was God's blessing for me as I got to experience some of the places and people of Russia outside of Moscow. For the many of my readers who probably have never experienced Russia first hand, let me say that it is an incredibly vast and complex country made up of many different people groups and cultures. Not only that, but the geography and climates of the old U.S.S.R. are as different as Arizona might be compared to Maine in the United States, or Alaska compared to Hawaii. It would probably surprise most people who think of Russia in terms of the deep winter snows depicted in the 'Dr. Zhivago' film that there are actually places in Russia with a sub tropical climate and palm trees like Florida! And so the opportunity to get at least a small glimpse of all this enriched my understanding of Mother Russia.

Looking back, though, the 'missionary guide' trip that impacted me the most was the one made to Greeyeznaberg, an industrial city located some distance southeast of Moscow. It was a very depressing city, as I recall. Everything there appeared to be covered over with a film of pollution. I say this not only in a natural sense as I was later told that various contaminants in this area made it unhealthy to physically live there, but also I speak here of a spiritual film. The death mantle of Communism had taken its toll on the inhabitants of this region. One could readily feel the spiritual heaviness that blanketed the area. Only the cleansing of the Gospel of Christ could remove this kind of spiritual oppression. I noted, though, that this cleansing process had indeed begun when I became acquainted with the newly formed church in Greeyeznaberg. Struggling for life, this humble body of young believers was the object of my missionary brothers' visit. It was this flickering beacon of hope that they sought out to encourage. I recognized that these two pastors I accompanied had come a great distance in order to encourage the hearts of the leadership in this young congregation as well as to show the love of Jesus in any other way that might be open to them. I was pleased that the Lord had permitted me to come along side them, though I wasn't so sure at first if they welcomed my presence. Let me explain.

My introduction to these two men was politely cordial, but not especially warm. I had been informed earlier by Pastor Shelter, who had been put in charge of the CGF church and office at the time that our visitors were not very happy about having to take me along, especially since this meant having to pay for my hotel room, ticket, and expenses. Apparently, word had not reached them beforehand that this was the new rule for all visiting CGF members. In many ways, I understood their objections, but nonetheless I was appointed to go and so wondered how I would be treated during the trip. I boarded the small Aeroflot plane in Moscow preparing myself to deal with the next few days ahead as the 'unwelcome' team member.

I can't underscore enough the heaviness that I felt in this city! But praise God, He lifted my spirits and raised me up above this difficult situation. Though my brothers were pretty much ignoring me, I was able to remain joyful and forgiving, even when I got left behind at the hospital we visited. This brings me to the high point of the visit and the focus of my story.

Pastor Stephen and Pastor Vance were noticeably disappointed when we arrived at the local hospital in Greeyeznaberg. While we all stood around at the hospital gate gazing at the numerous patients who had been packed into the hospital courtyard by nursing staff, we listened intently as our interpreter explained what the hospital official, who stood in front of us, was saying. He informed us that we would be allowed to pray with the patients who had gathered outside of the building, but we would not be allowed to go inside the hospital during our visit. I looked around again. It was so strange to think that all of these sick people had been sent outside to greet us. Only those who absolutely couldn't get out of bed were left inside! As I looked up at the top of this five or six story building, I noted another strange phenomenon. There were actually some patients sitting on open window ledges! Some sat kitty corner with their backs against one side of the window frame while others dared to sit in a forward position, dangling their legs over the ledge. I held my breath as I thought about some poor weak patient losing his balance and falling from such a height. I further entertained a rather serious thought...were these two pastors I accompanied prepared to resurrect the dead should this worst case scenario occur?

The two pastors exchanged some words with each other and decided that a brief message should first be delivered to the patients who were eagerly watching to see what these foreigners would do. One of the pastors shared a little bit from his heart and then we all proceeded to start praying with this one and that one in the courtyard. As is my habit, I closed my eyes to block out any distractions as I sought the Lord for each one. At last, I came to one patient who insisted that I go inside to pray for a seriously sick friend who was bedridden. The young man from the church who was with me helped me to explain that we were not permitted to go inside, but the next thing I knew, I had been given special permission to enter the building and was brought to the bedside of the very sick friend. That was the beginning of maybe two hours of praying with many patients inside of the hospital. No sooner would I finish with one, than another would motion me to come. As time melted away with all of the praying, I found myself so high in the Spirit and lost in prayer that I totally lost track of the two pastors who were praying outside. They apparently finished up some time sooner than I did and returned to their hotel room escorted by their interpreters. The rather amusing part of the story is that they had totally forgotten that I was there with them! So, like the little boy in the movie who got forgotten at home when his parents and siblings went on vacation, I got left behind. Once my young friend and I realized what had happened, we made our way to the street and started to walk back to the hotel. Fortunately, the young man was aware of what hotel I was booked in or I would really have been lost. Anyway, I took it all in stride, not quite understanding how these two men could totally forget that I had been with them, but at the same time not holding anything against them for the error.

When I arrived back at the hotel, the two pastors apologized for leaving me behind. They had been quite worried when they realized what they had done and both of them were noticeably embarrassed that I had been so ignored that I ended up being totally forgotten when they left the hospital with their interpreters. I really tried to make them feel at ease about the situation, even though perhaps the Lord was using it to call them to account for their poor attitude about bringing me along. As I sat with them that evening in the hotel restaurant helping them to order their meals, the ice was at last broken! I finally became accepted by my two charges and so the rest of the trip was much more pleasant.

Before leaving this story, I need to share with the reader that while in Russia, I had a number of occasions to visit patients inside the hospitals. Most of these medical facilities were grossly inadequate by modern standards. The hospital in Greeyeznaberg, typical of what I had seen, was no exception. As I entered the building it was like stepping back at least fifty years in time! The patient beds, resembling army cots, were low to the ground. Basic modern medical equipment one would normally expect to see was obviously lacking, and as in most of the hospitals, bed linens and food had to be brought in by the patient's family. What impacted me the most about this particular hospital was that there were a number of patients walking about who had had some kind of major brain surgery. All I could think of was that some kind of lobotomy had been performed or perhaps some other form of experimental surgery. At any rate, whatever had been done and why, the resulting disfigurements to the head were extreme with deep impressions in the skull or a portion of the head missing. My heart went out to the five or six patients I saw who walked about with this kind of condition. I will always retain a picture of this hospital and the patients, especially these, in my heart and mind.

My discussion of the CGF church in Moscow and my first year in Russia wouldn't be complete without talking about the worship team that bussed into Moscow from a city that was about two hours away. Because our musicians were imported for the weekend, they needed to be put up somewhere on Saturday nights. The young men on the team normally had a regular place to stay, but Tatyana, the only female member of the worship team could not, of course, be put up with the guys and so I was asked to be her hostess during the weekends. This actually turned out to be a great pleasure for me as I not only became a very close friend with my Russian sister, but I also eventually got to sing with the Russian team from time to time. My association with these young professional musicians was almost always a delight and a welcome relief from the internal conflicts that seemed to be continually surfacing among my fellow missionaries. Yes, the worship team members were always quite gracious and a lot of fun to be around. As time went on, they welcomed me as one of their own, forgetting from time to time that I was their American sister who spoke a little bit of 'funny' Russian.

I'll never forget the first time that I met Tatyana. She was a pretty young woman, being about ten years my junior, and someone who was always bubbling over with energy. She had been a fairly well known female pop vocalist in some parts of Russia and the Ukraine before she met Jesus. I must say that God gave her one of the clearest, most beautiful voices I have ever heard before or since and a heart of gold to go with it! Our spirits became knit together almost immediately despite the language and cultural differences. I'll always remember our initial introduction as I brought her to my apartment for the first time. We met at the end of the worship team's Saturday practice session and then made our way to the bus stop. Sitting together for the twenty-minute ride, all we could do was to smile at each other and giggle. This was due to my lack of speaking Russian in those earlier days and her inability to communicate in English. Eventually, I started to pick up more Russian, but until then our most important conversations necessitated a Russian-English dictionary and a little bit of patience!

Another experience that will always be etched in my memory was my trip to the Ukraine. Our Moscow worship team had been invited to conduct the praise and worship at one particular Bible school there. When Anatoli, the team's sound man, and Tatyana invited me to join them for a week, I gladly went through the ordeal of securing a special visa to go. Getting this visa was no easy task considering the local bureaucracy, but by the following week everything was prepared and so I boarded one of the green Russian overnight trains with the members of the music group. This was to be my first experience on a Russian train and because the trip took about one and a half days, there was plenty of time to enjoy my new friends.

Our traveling compartment had four narrow bunks, two up and two down. Tatyana and I took the top berths that jutted out from opposite walls of the cabin. Two of the men slept on the bottom bunks. This was the arrangement for sleeping, but while we traveled during waking hours, everyone sat on the bottom bunks that were stripped of their bed linens to serve as daytime seating. This was the custom while riding the trains. The other custom I learned was to bring along bread, cheese and perhaps some salami to eat during the trip. There was one railway car that served food, but it was expensive and almost no one used this little traveler's restaurant. Periodically, the train would stop to let off passengers and so it was possible then to purchase basic food items from local vendors who would sell things like warm 'bliney', (Russian crepes or pancakes), with a potato filling, apples, drinks, and whatever food was appropriate for the travelers. One had to be careful, though, not to purchase or bring along food that would spoil because there was no refrigeration available on the trains. I do have to say that this was a stretch for my American understanding of food preservation! Back in the States, I would never have considered eating salami or cheese that had sat out in the heat for a day or two, nor would I have drank out of community glasses that had been rinsed in cold water and then passed on to the next thirsty customer! But this was another time and another place, and so I just prayed a lot and managed to stay remarkably healthy during most of my stay in Russia.

I must say that traveling with a group of Russians when you can barely speak their language can be a challenge, and even a bit frustrating if one doesn't adopt the right attitude. Only Anatoli had a minimum ability to speak English at that time and I could tell that he easily got weary of translating what was being said. Later on, I understood a little better how tiring it can be to translate Russian into English and vice-versa, especially when one only has a minimal ability to flow in a second language. But back then, I found it a bit difficult to miss out on the finer details of what was being spoken! And so during that first train ride, I had to be content to put my frustrations aside and do my best to follow the conversations on my own. Considering my lack of Russian in those early days of my adventures, I somehow managed to comprehend and communicate the basics. This was due not to any natural ability of my own, but to God's grace alone and so I give Him the glory for being my Translator!

My one night on the train was not the most productive in terms of sleep, but it was definitely good for my heart as Tatyana and I attempted some light-hearted communication between our bunks in the upper reaches of the cabin. Though she was in her thirties and I was ten years her senior, we acted more like young school girls at a slumber party. I'm not sure how well this settled with the two young men under us who were trying to get some sleep, but there were not any complaints made, or at least I should say that I didn't understand any complaints if they did indeed occur! The upper berths that we slept on were narrow, causing one to 'toss and turn' with great care for fear of making a crash landing below. In fact, this too was a major hindrance to sleep because during slumber it was more likely that an uncalculated move could be made, resulting in a fall. At any rate, our night watch on the train began with quite a stir as Tatyana sprang from her bunk all the while screaming frantically, "Tarakon, Tarakon!" Not having any idea what she was saying, the Russian word sounded to me more like "Dragon, Dragon!" After her bunk was checked and she quietly settled back into her sleeping compartment, it was explained to me that the object of Tatyana's fear was not a 'dragon' but a 'cockroach'! This bit of comedy only fueled the fire for the two 'school girls' as my Russian sister burst out in delightful laughter when she learned about my initial interpretation of 'tarakon'. Of course, I had to join her in the merriment...I'm afraid that for our cabin mates it turned out to be a very long night.

My short visit at the Bible school passed too quickly. It was so exciting to be with the students that week and to see their reactions to the worship services and what was being taught. These were a select group of new believers who had been sent by the leadership of various churches throughout Russia and the Ukraine to receive introductory and intense training in the Word of God for a period of several months. When their session had ended, they would then be sent back to their respective home churches to help light some new fires among the lost sheep of the Russian population. The legacy of seventy years of Communism had caused a great hunger among the students for Truth and for the Word of God, which is after all, the embodiment of all Truth. Like many of the Russian believers these young people were evangelistic, on fire, and ready to believe every Word that God had spoken. When one of these tender lambs asked for prayer to be healed, you knew that they had the faith to receive God's healing. When there was a call to repent or change their ways, there was almost always a pliable lump of clay for the Great Potter to work with. The competition and jealousy that too often resulted in the American churches that I had been a part of seemed to be refreshingly absent. Perhaps the enemy came in and this kind of spirit developed later on, but at least in the beginning, the dictates of Communism did have one good effect. This positive side of such an ungodly system can be described as the breaking down of the 'me' mentality, enabling its adherents to work together as a team. The more developed churches in America and elsewhere could learn many lessons in this regard from the new believers that they were reaching out to in Russia and the Ukraine.

At the end of my visit at the Bible school, Tatyana and Anatoli brought me to the train station and helped me to locate my cabin and bunk for the return trip to Moscow. They needed to stay on and so I settled myself inside my assigned cabin, ready to fare the return journey alone. Actually, despite all the many unknowns, I thought that it might be a little more restful on this return trip. I wouldn't have to work so hard to communicate because my new cabin mates would be strangers and therefore I could just 'tune out', excusing myself because of the language problem. That would leave me free to rest, sleep and ponder my own thoughts about the previous visit. It was a nice tidy thought I had, but my plans for the ride back were obviously not God's plans! In walked a robust grandmother, ("Babushka" in Russian), her adult son in his late thirties, and her grandson of about twelve. That took care of the three empty bunks...but wait a minute, an additional ticket holder entered our cabin...a middle-aged businessman from India, a Hindu, who as it turned out happened to be fluent in both English and Russian. Yes, the hours ahead would prove to be more than interesting for 'yours truly'!

Chapter Eleven

"The Man from India"

As I nestled into my seat inside the train compartment, I thought about the events of the past five or six months. Yes, it was quite a miracle to be in Russia doing what I was doing! Just a few short years ago I would have thought that the reality of such a thing actually coming to pass would be next to impossible. It's true that I was believing God for this opportunity of serving Him outside of my own country, yet such a giant step of faith hadn't taken on reality in my life until this very time and season. Marveling at such a thing, though, I had to acknowledge that here I was! And once again, the evidence was before me that the 'God of the impossible' had acted on my behalf by sending me to this far away place. More and more the impossible, and yes, the abnormal and the unusual, was becoming a part of my everyday life. I was keenly aware of the fact that I could never view life in the same way again after seeing God move so supernaturally in my behalf. It was as though I was living in a different dimension or realm from most of the people around me. They lived their lives and made their decisions according to the world's natural law, while I believed and lived according to God's Law, His Word…which is after all 'supernatural law'! Indeed, it truly was a supernatural realm I was beginning to move about in, a place where you call things into being, according to God's Word to you, 'things that were not as if they were', and they become reality in your life. My thoughts began to culminate with this revelation: At last I was learning to use the 'keys' that Jesus had given to Peter and to all believers! These were the keys that opened the door to the Kingdom, making it possible to understand the mystery of what it means to live in this 'Kingdom of God', as Jesus called it. Remarkably, His Kingdom was beginning to be revealed to me as a place where faith in God and His Word, rather than fear in man and circumstances, rules one's life. I knew that I still had a long ways to go with this faith adventure, but my understanding of

Kingdom principles was definitely growing.

"And I also say to you that you are Peter, and on this rock I will build My church, and the gates of Hades shall not prevail against it. And I will give you the keys of the kingdom of heaven, and whatever you bind on earth will be bound in heaven, and whatever you loose on earth will be loosed in heaven." (Matthew 16:18 &19)

My thoughts drifted back to what was happening in the train car as our latest arrival, the businessman from India, introduced himself to me in English. I think that he was nearly as surprised to see me in this setting as I was to see him. He conversed a bit with me and then switched over to Russian to talk with the Babushka and her adult son. As the Babushka eyed me with a kind of curiosity that not only sizes up appearance but also attempts to probe the very nature of one's soul, the questions started coming. Where are you from? What are you doing in Russia? Why would anyone from such a wealthy country want to be here? The man from India was only too happy to translate this conversation as it went back and forth. I could sense an opening at this point to begin sharing the Gospel as I observed the Babushka listening intently to what I said; even her son started to ask questions. I looked at my new Indian friend and wondered how he was actually interpreting all of this. After all, he was admittedly Hindu and perhaps, I thought, he would take advantage of this situation to alter my words.

The ride back to Moscow passed rather quickly. We all shared whatever food items had been brought along for the trip, turning what could be a tedious journey into a festive and party-like occasion. Part of that Russian spirit of celebration included a bottle of some sort of homemade liquor that was pulled out of the Indian man's sack. He told us that this had been given to him as a present from some of his contacts in the Ukraine. I eyed the bottle cautiously, wondering what exactly was inside. Perhaps it was some kind of wine, or maybe even vodka. As the glasses were set out on our little cabin table, there was great pressure put on me to join in the numerous toasts that were made while the fiery liquid was rapidly gulped down. I really didn't want to imbibe, but felt that I at least needed to show some respect for their traditions by taking just a little. I can report to you that the taste was horrible beyond description, far worse than some terrible homemade potato wine that friends of my parents had brewed years earlier! I caught my breath after my introductory sip and with great difficulty managed to get excused from drinking anymore.

The rest of the trip was uneventful until the train was maybe an hour away from its destination in Moscow. It was at this time that I began to realize that the Lord had a two-fold purpose in my Gospel outreach! I had focused so strongly on my Russian travel companions that I was totally unaware of how my testimony and God's Word had stirred up some things in the heart of the Indian businessman! I tried to contain my excitement as he asked me where I went to church in Moscow. After writing down directions and the time of the service, he promised to pay a visit to our Russian congregation on the following Sunday.

To end this little story, the 'following Sunday' came around quickly, and from my position on the stage where I joined our worship team in their Russian rendition of the chorus, "Alive, Alive, Alive forevermore ...My Jesus is Alive, He's Alive forevermore", I carefully watched who entered our service. As this one and that one came into the large theater space that our church rented on Sunday mornings, I strained to see if my man from India would make good on his promise to visit us. At last, I saw him come in and take a seat in one of the middle rows. The service itself progressed from praise and worship, to some quick announcements, to the preaching of the Word. This particular morning the message was given and then the Lord's Supper followed. Though an altar call was not specifically made at this time, Pastor Shelter clearly explained to the congregation that the one requirement for partaking of the Body and Blood of Christ was that one needed to believe in Jesus. He explained that it was necessary for this profession of faith to take place in one's heart with the understanding that Jesus was indeed the true Son of the Living God, sent for the forgiveness of sins, thus making salvation possible for all who believed. In the way that Pastor Shelter gave explanation to the congregation, there could be no misunderstanding of Who Jesus was and what He did for us. The man from India not only heard all of this in English, but he got a double portion of the Word as he heard it translated into Russian. I watched with great expectancy as the Russian sheep filed down to the front to participate in the Lord's Supper...then I spotted one lone Indian sheep among them! My heart rejoiced to see what an unusual and miraculous thing the Lord had orchestrated during my return trip to Moscow. I have heard it said that 'salvation' is the greatest miracle of all. And so my wonderful God had acted in the life of this Indian businessman in a very supernatural way. Yes, on this very day he had had his first encounter with the God of Abraham, Isaac and Jacob. The One True God Who had revealed Himself to the dying world in the Person of Jesus, the Messiah, had supernaturally spoken to this man's heart. I could almost hear the angels in heaven rejoicing with me as the man from India experienced his first true encounter with a supernatural God!

Chapter Twelve

"The Pastor's Conference & The Map Dream"

The next four or five months marked a time of transition for me once again. I had left Moscow, resettling in Stolitsa, a large city several hours away. There I planned to travel by train on the weekends to a small outlying town called Petrushka where I would assist one young pastor with a new work. Pastor Victor was in his early 40's, but had only come to the Lord just a year or so before. He was hungry for the Word of God and anxious to serve the sheep, but still needed some backup for a while as he grew into his assigned task. For the reader who is not familiar with the situation in the newly formed Russian churches that emerged just after Peristroika, let it be said that men who were just cutting their eye teeth on the things of God were often placed in positions of authority in the church. Before they had a chance to mature as believers, they would be called on to shepherd their young flocks because no pool of seasoned pastors existed. The church in Russia was fresh and new and so too was most of its leadership!

During these months, I took the commuter train each week to Petrushka and did a home fellowship group there that focused on laying a foundation in the Word of God. Sometimes I also did the Sunday morning service, though I really tried not to interfere with too much of the 'doing' so that Victor would begin to gain some confidence and develop in his role as pastor. I saw myself merely as a temporary facilitator in this young congregation, knowing that most of us who were sent into the old U.S.S.R. after its breakup were there only for a season. It was our job to assist with the birth process and 'wet nurse' the young believers with the milk of God's Word. After that, we needed to recognize that a weaning time would follow when the Russian church would naturally begin to stand on its own. As the 90's drew to a close, this indeed happened. The first churches that had been established in the larger population centers were ready to send out their own missionaries into the many more remote cities, towns, and villages of this vast country.

When I wasn't in Petrushka, I gave great time and attention to my Russian language studies. For two months, I was able to get some help from a university professor in Stolitsa, but she charged me about $200 a month for her services…an extremely high fee, especially back then. On my missionary budget, at that price I couldn't afford to continue for long. This was the only formal study I ever had in the Russian language. Other than that, I just kept plugging away on my own with this very complicated language. Because of the complex grammar structure, I was told that Russian ranked third from the top in difficulty. After struggling with Russian grammar for awhile, I definitely came into agreement with this statement!

During the week, I also did a second Bible Study/Home Group with the Moscow worship team members who resided in Stolitsa. This never really took hold the way that I had hoped it would. In fact, I actually found myself becoming a bit disappointed in some of these young musicians because they seemed more interested in fellowshipping than in gaining knowledge in the Word of God. The worship team members, all of them brand new Christians, had been excessively pampered and highly paid to lead worship by an earlier regime of missionaries in the Moscow church. This, in some ways, was a great detriment to their earlier growth as believers. Knowing some of the events and situations that followed in their lives, three and possibly four of them continued to grow in the Lord and to be used in His Kingdom business in Russia and the Ukraine. The others eventually fell by the wayside, going back to 'business as usual', conducting their lives the way they did before Jesus had been invited in.

I need to pause here for a moment to weave another colorful thread into this part of my story, a very delicate 'matter of the heart' that emerged at this time causing some real struggles.

This was the episode of romance that the enemy meant for evil, but that God, in all of His Wisdom and foreknowledge, used for good. This was a very difficult time for me as the enemy used it not only to distract me but also to crush me with the surfacing of strong emotions that I hadn't experienced for such a long time. After all, it had been about 15 years since the marriage of my youth fell apart so I was greatly affected by the attention and gestures of love that came my way. I could go on about this episode, but I think that it's enough to say that despite all of my constant prayers and seeking God about this situation with much pain and endless tears, He did not permit a marriage to take place. Looking back, I can breathe a sign of relief and say, "Thank You Father", because once I pulled myself away from the situation, the gray clouds that were blinding the eyes of my heart were swept away. I recognized only too well that a marriage to this man would have been a total disaster that would have altered, and possibly totally disrupted, the future plans that my Heavenly Father had for me.

This fleeting romance was the last thing that I expected to happen while I was in Russia, but I can say that I learned a number of lessons from it. The most important lesson was that God, in all of His tender love and mercy, would not permit me to walk totally into the enemy's trap if I kept myself open to hear Him and to respond to 'His Final Word' about my situation. Too often we think that we, ourselves, should have the final word and so we close our minds to the possibility that God may have a totally different plan for us. Often this may mean taking an alternate route to our destination, while at other times, the Holy Spirit may be requiring us to proceed in a totally different direction! We must remain sensitive to the Voice of God and be willing to act on His instructions. Herein lies our protection from getting off track with God's purposes for our lives…being ever ready 'to listen' and 'to obey'! I can remember that my pleading prayers for a marriage to take place always reluctantly ended with the conditional clause, "Lord if for some reason this isn't Your will for me, then so be it"…and so it was! Shortly after the pastor's conference in Stolitsa had ended, one that I had been asked to help organize, I moved onto God's next destination for me, leaving my potential marriage partner behind. It wasn't easy to separate myself from this relationship, but it had become clear to me after all the struggling, that I would be disobedient to continue. And so I reprogrammed my heart and my mind and waited for clarification on God's next set of orders.

As I alluded to earlier, the CGF had decided to put on a pastor's conference in Stolitsa at one of the hotels there and asked me if I would be willing to take care of making the arrangements. They explained to me that many pastors and church leaders from all over Russia and the Ukraine would be invited to attend this gathering, along with a smaller number of pastors and missionaries from the States. I guardedly offered my assistance. When the time for the conference came around it was necessary for me, as one of the coordinators, to be present as well. My attitude, I have to confess, about attending this conference was neither 'hot' nor 'cold' and so I selectively attended a few of its seminars and managed to slip out early when the teaching or preaching failed to hold my interest. But despite my lukewarm disposition, God used the pastor's conference and one particular Russian Jewish brother who was in attendance, as His agent to activate a dream that I had had maybe two weeks before the conference took place. As I go ahead and relay the contents of my dream to you, I must say that I love to share this part of my story because it demonstrates with great clarity how the Spirit of God supernaturally leads and guides us.

In an effort to describe this dream, I must first say that it depicted a map of Europe and Asia that was colored in with mostly greens and browns. I noted a kind of line or boundary somewhere in the middle of the map and recognized that this was the dividing line that marked the boundary between the continent of Europe and the continent of Asia. As my attention was keenly focused on this line, there were instructions given to me. I was told in my dream that I would be sent to an area of Russia that, "was as far as one could go while still remaining in the European portion of Russia". I awoke from the dream realizing that it was a very unusual dream, a map dream, and that it contained information regarding my next Divine assignment. Recognizing that the instructions in my dream came from the Spirit of God, I heeded what was said as I carefully tucked the dream away in my spirit, waiting all the while until I would receive some further revelation. This revelation was given to me a couple of weeks later during the pastor's conference. God was faithful to provide the green light that I needed to act on what was spoken.

During one of the morning conference sessions, Pastor Mill's assistant spoke. It was a simple, but strong message about God's love for us. As he expounded on this topic, he asked one of the men to come to the front of the room. I eagerly watched as a chair was placed in the center of the platform area. A rather pleasant, short, Russian man smiled as he sat down. He was likened to God the Father. Then his young son of about five years was invited to come up front and to sit in his daddy's lap. Something about this man's countenance caught my attention! Later on while we were all waiting around for the hotel to serve our lunch, I struck up a conversation with him. I learned that his name was Yuri and that he was Jewish and a deacon in his church in one coastal city located in southern Russia. I also learned that Yuri had eight children, something very unusual for most Russian couples who normally had only one or two. As our exchange of words in Russian continued, I pressed him to explain a little more about where his city and church was located in relation to Moscow.

By the time that the doors had opened to welcome the conference members inside the banquet room for lunch, I started to get a strong witness from the Holy Spirit that this man came from the area that God was directing me to in my dream. Sure enough, as I went home to sleep that night, I checked in my atlas to see where Sonskaya was actually located. There it was, right on the broken boundary line that separated European from Asian Russia! I mused with great gladness in my heart because this man, too, was Jewish! He symbolized the inner knowledge deep inside of my being that all of this had to do with those earlier promptings of the Spirit, preparing me for the day that I would be working with Russian Jewish immigrants who would be part of the 'second Exodus' into Israel. I can't even begin to describe the emotions and excitement that flooded my soul as some of the Divine puzzle pieces began to come together. The next day at the conference, I sought Yuri out and there were arrangements made to visit his city and congregation. I knew that I had to "go" and "see", and that God would give me further instructions during my visit to Sonskaya. Two weeks later, I once again found myself boarding a Russian train. Together with my interpreter, we journeyed many kilometers to the south and the east of Stolitsa. It was time to 'spy out the land' and to see what the Holy Spirit would show me. Yes, God was leading me down His supernatural path. My current spiritual adventure with Him had only just begun!

Chapter Thirteen

"Discovering the Port & Exodus II"

"Therefore the days are coming," says the Lord, "that it shall no more be said, 'The Lord lives who brought up the children of Israel from the land of Egypt,' but, 'The Lord lives who brought up the children of Israel from the land of the north and from all the lands where He had driven them.' For I will bring them back into their land which I gave to their fathers." (Jeremiah 16: 14 & 15)

The train ride was quite lengthy, being a day and a half journey to Sonskaya from Moscow, but somehow the time passed quickly and at last we were there. Yuri had arranged for us to stay with one prominent family in his city. The husband happened to be the director of the police force there as well as a leader in Yuri's church. Though our arrival was late in the day and we were weary from all of the traveling, Anatoli, my interpreter, and I were obliged to accept the Russian hospitality lavished on us by our host and hostess. And so around midnight, we were feasting on various Russian-style hors d'oeuvres and discussing the situation for the Jews who called this coastal region of southern Russia 'Home'. Our host had gone so far as to arrange some airtime on their local television station for me to talk about the current Exodus of the Soviet Jews, (those from the "land of the north"), into Israel! You might ask, why the designation the "land of the north"? Take a look at an atlas and you will see that a straight line can be drawn from Jerusalem northward to Moscow. A large number of Jews had settled in these northern lands throughout the Diaspora, (those Jews who had been expelled and dispersed from their native homeland, Israel.) So to return to the TV spot that had been arranged, I knew with certainty in my spirit that this would be 'jumping the gun' on whatever God was currently doing with me. Besides, I was totally unprepared to address the viewers on this topic. After all, I had just arrived in this region and I was waiting to see what the Lord would speak to me regarding my part in serving those Russian Jews who would be part of the second Exodus.

While in Sonskaya, I visited Yuri's congregation and later met with one Jewish couple who wanted to make aliyah, (to immigrate into Israel). Their only stumbling block at this point of the aliyah process was financial. Money was needed to get their papers processed for entry into Israel. I felt that I had just enough money to get me where I needed to go during this trip, but knew that I had to sow something into their aliyah. It wasn't a lot, but I pulled out a $50 bill, gave it to them, and told God that I was definitely trusting Him for my supply! The reader needs to understand that during this time period in Russia that a foreigner couldn't just go to a bank and take out a cash advance on his or her credit card. Neither was the mail delivery system into Russia dependable, and even if it had been, a check mailed to a foreigner in Russia was not cashable. So, the only system that worked for the missionaries was for cash in dollars to be hand-carried into Russia by Christian brothers or sisters who came to visit. My 'supply' always came this way via the CGF office in Moscow. But I never knew how much money would come in or how often someone would be making a trip to Moscow from the States. So, as you can see, God was putting all of my earlier 'raven food' training into practice. In fact, as I sit here in Jerusalem the 'raven food' drop-offs continue but with a more modern delivery system. God is always faithful!

After staying in Sonskaya for about two days, I recognized that this was not the place that God was sending me so I decided to head southward to another coastal town that also had a sizeable port of entry for ships. There were actually three of these 'port' cities on this strip of coastline as I learned during my trip. The fascination with a port city had to do with something else that the Holy Spirit had tucked inside of me...that I would be somehow involved with helping Jews who would return to Israel by ship. To this day I can't explain how this knowledge came to me. I just knew it!

The bus ride to Portgarad, though six or seven hours long was more of an ordeal than the lengthy train ride from Moscow. Anatoli and I had to stand part of the way and the springtime heat was already getting intense in this sub-tropical area of Russia. Our bus, as was the case for most vehicles of transport in Russia, had no air conditioning. The narrow bumpy road that we traveled curved and twined its way up hill and down for most of the trip; it was like taking a roller coaster ride in slow motion. Finally after reaching our destination, despite the rough journey, I quickly revived because of the anticipation of what I might soon discover. I wasn't disappointed.

"Anatoli", I excitedly requested, "we need to find the port and to call this one lady that Yuri gave us as a possible contact." The port was easy to find because Anatoli had been to this city before and had a pretty good idea about where things were located. I'll never forget my amazement as we approached the port area. My gaze became almost frozen as I looked out at the vast expanse of sea with its blue-gray waters. It felt so large and without boundaries, yet I knew that eventually there was a southern shoreline that embraced Turkey and an entryway into the Mediterranean Sea. From there, Israel became accessible to those Jews whose hearts were turning them toward home. My gaze became unfixed on the waters as my attention was next drawn to the outdoor ticket booth. Anatoli and I approached the cassa, the cashier, to inquire about any boats scheduled to leave for Israel. Knowing that boats from this port made regular runs into Turkey, it was logical for me to think that boats also sailed to Israel from here.

The cassa shook her head 'no' as Anatoli made the inquiry for me. She looked a bit perplexed to think that such a thing existed, that is, a boat from Portgarad going to Israel? Well, I

93

wasn't going to settle for her answer. Surely she must be mistaken, I thought, or she's just doing her best to be 'unhelpful' as was the case with some of the Russian cassas. So I looked around and spotted a little kiosk off to the side. Expecting that the kiosk vender would know most of what was going on at the port, I called upon Anatoli once again to ask the vital question about the boat to Israel. This time the response was even less polite...the kiosk vender tried to brush us off as being a bit crazy for asking such a thing! Receiving these negative answers still didn't discourage me. I just knew that there would be some kind of a boat bound for Israel, if not from this port, from another port on this coastline. God had somehow led me to understand this and so I stubbornly held on to my revelation.

With our backs to the sea, we started to retrace our steps through the passenger waiting area. A public telephone needed to be located to make a call to Yuri's contact. I cranked my head around for a moment looking for one...and then it hit me. "How could I have missed it", the words sprang from my lips! My thoughts turned inward as I slipped into the realm of my night visions. What I saw before me was not the empty park benches that had escaped my notice as we approached the port less than an hour ago, but instead these concrete-poured structures that seated busy passengers who were about to be boarded onto a ship. Some sat while others milled about the grassy knoll. There were 'babushkas', grandmothers, in simple cotton print dresses, wearing kerchiefs that were snuggly wrapped and tied at the nap of the neck. Their long cotton stockings bunched at the ankles as they fluctuated from tending to their bundles and bags to talking somewhat anxiously with family and friends who would soon be left behind. One long-bearded old gentleman, hands clasped behind him, paced back and forth in deep contemplation while his unmarried daughter called to him from a distance. Families representing a mixture of generations, as well as a few singles, clutched onto their loved ones as well as their limited worldly belongings. I couldn't help but recognize that the scene that I was picturing was as real as the ground I stood on, though it was scheduled to happen sometime in the future. I switched back to the present reality of the empty benches lining the port. One thing was abundantly clear. This was the place that I had seen in one of the segments of my four-part dream, the dream that I had had before entering the missionary training school, and the very same dream that contained the Russian market scene. There was no doubt in my heart that this would be the port that Russian Jewish immigrants would depart from as they made their way into Israel. "Anatoli", I beckoned, "we still haven't found a telephone. Perhaps there'll be one on our way into town."

We were never able to reach Ludmila that day, but were relieved when she was at home to answer her phone the next morning. This was the contact that Yuri had given me while I was in Sonskaya. Later that day, we met and I learned that she was a kind of mission's coordinator for her church, a large charismatic congregation that was only two years old and about eight hundred in number. Ludmila also told me that she was Jewish and that she had been in contact with one ministry in Europe that had secured a large naval ship. They were currently putting the final touches on restoring the ship and equipping it to accommodate some very precious cargo, Soviet Jews who were bound for Israel! My ears perked up as she shared her secret, informing me that she was the only one in the region aware of these plans. Not only that, but this ministry was currently praying and talking with officials in three different port cities along the coast to determine where the Lord was basing the boat ministry. Sonskaya and another nearby port city were being considered along with Portgarad. When I told Ludmila what the Holy Spirit had revealed to me, she too was surprised. "Ludmila", I spoke through my interpreter with great excitement, "I know that Portgarad is going to be that city! Do you think that you could help me locate an apartment?"

Chapter Fourteen

"Settling In & Getting Ready for the Ship"

Thus says the Lord God:
"Behold, I will lift up My hand in an oath to the nations,
And set up My standard for the peoples;
They shall bring your sons in their arms,
And your daughters shall be carried on their shoulders;"
(Isaiah 49:22)

The verse quoted above is just one of many to be found among the Old Testament prophets telling about the re-gathering of Israel. Yes, long ago, God had spoken about the return of His dispersed children, those Jews who had been scattered among the Nations. They would be brought back to Israel in the latter days. Their return would herald in the greatest event of this passing away age, the return of Yeshua, the Messiah of not only Israel, but of all those who put their trust in Him as the 'Anointed One', the 'Son of the Living God'! The Gentiles, those believers from the Nations, would have a special part in helping the children of Jacob return to their 'Promised Land'. Some of the sons and daughters would be flown to Israel by plane, while others would choose to go by ship. What a marvelous thing it was to have a part in all of this! I knew that I was about to move right into the center of Biblical prophecy as it was being fulfilled. Somehow, I would be a participant in what my wonderful God was doing in this amazing end time event!

* * * * * * * * * * *

The sky was blue and the air was washed clean by the salty breezes of the nearby sea. I peered out through a large paned window near the wooden kitchen table. From high on a hill sat my temporary residence in Portgarad; I had only two weeks to locate a more permanent apartment. The current living quarters were lovely, but far too expensive for my budget, and as I later would

97

learn, not conducive to the home cell group setting that would soon be needed. Ludmila, my one and only contact in Portgarad, had tried to find some normal housing for me, but thus far had been unsuccessful. But as usual, I didn't need to panic. God had it all worked out!

Portgarad was made up of a series of mountains and hills. Except for the low-lying area of the sea, everything either went sharply up or steeply down. Flat level spaces were at a premium. There had always been a little bit of 'mountain goat' in me and so I welcomed this new opportunity to get into shape as I made my daily hikes into town. A couple of days after I had arrived in Portgarad, I met one young couple who were volunteers with a well-known International Christian organization. They had been renting a comfortable studio apartment in an older apartment complex just two hundred and eighty-seven stairs below me! As we got acquainted and they learned that I needed some permanent housing very soon, they were only too delighted to tell me that in another week or so they'd be moving out and that their apartment would be available. About ten days later, I found myself making a number of trips down the hill, dragging my worldly belongings behind me as my overstuffed rolling duffle bags bumped over the lengthy staircase to my newly secured apartment. Once settled into my cozy abode, I would remain there for over two-thirds of my appointed time in Portgarad.

I quickly won favor with my new landlady and neighbors. Despite the fact that I was a foreigner, I always felt safe in my apartment and well accepted by the other tenants. It was a real blessing that no one ever complained about the extra noise and activity when my weekly cell group of twenty-five to thirty people packed into my little apartment. I couldn't help but recognize that God had handpicked this spot for me as a base to operate from. And just as He had so perfectly planted me in this apartment, He almost immediately settled me into the large Russian charismatic church that Ludmila attended, giving me great favor with the

Russian pastor there. During our first meeting, I was invited to carry out the vision for Jewish ministry that the Lord had given to me under the spiritual covering of this church, and in that context, I became the 'American' Jewish ministry leader in a Russian church! I can't explain the strong bonding, love, and trust that existed almost from the beginning of my time there in Portgarad because it was truly from God and it was definitely supernatural! The kind of relationships that I had with the pastor, leadership of the church, and the sheep normally take years to develop. But it was as though I had come to Portgarad 'walking on water' and the sheep couldn't do enough to help me promote and propagate God's work there regarding the Jew. I've never experienced the likes of this before or after, even in the Lakelands where I enjoyed great favor with the real sheep. In fact, I must tell you that I had to be very careful not to let my flesh glory in all of the attention and respect many of these sheep gave me. The Lord had endowed me with a goodly measure of authority during this time for the purpose of getting the job done, and because of this I had to watch myself closely, taking care to remain humble and submitted.

My home cell group, which was one among ten or twelve such groups in this young thriving church, was unique in that it was made up almost equally of Jewish and Gentile believers. Only those who had a strong desire to minister to the local Jewish population were encouraged to participate in this cell group. The focus of our group was to inform the many Jews in the local community about the Scriptures regarding the 'Second Exodus' and to encourage them to make aliyah to Israel. There was also the hope, of course, that perhaps our Jewish brothers and sisters would meet Yeshua, their Messiah, in the process and some of them did!

How I loved being in Portgarad. I got to be a spiritual mother or big sister to more than a few of the believers who were brand new miracles, just recently being birthed into the Kingdom. This relationship existed mostly with the folks in my home group, but I realized later that a number of the young home group leaders, most of them remarkably only one or two years old in the Lord themselves, were also looking to me for advice, prayer, and encouragement. All of these young leaders, plus a large group from the congregation, attended a newly established Bible school sponsored by the church. Meeting in the evening several times a week, the school was directed by Amari and his wife, Vera, who were from neighboring Armenia. As I would understand about five years later, this couple had truly been sent to this area of coastal Russia, not only for the purpose of teaching in and establishing a Bible school, but later to lay the groundwork for a vital aliyah ministry. This aliyah outreach would be based in Portgarad, but would extend well beyond the Portgarad region. This is yet one more fantastic story and miracle that the Lord orchestrated and put me right in the middle of, but I'm getting ahead of myself once again...

Four or five months had passed since the Lord had established me in Portgarad. My home cell group was in full swing by this time. In fact, my living room and adjoining porch were so packed with people that I quickly ran out of furniture for seating my guests. Graciously, my enthusiastic Russian brothers and sisters never complained once about having to sit on blankets or pillows on the hard wooden floor. Because their main objective was to take in the Word of God, I gladly taught them all that the Lord placed on my heart, praying with them and discipling them with the hope that God's plan of redemption for both Jew and Gentile would be firmly established within them. And to that end, I also prayed that they would have a deep understanding of the inseparable family connection between Judaism and Christianity. In addition to this, I sought to explain God's plan to restore the sons and daughters of Jacob back to both physical and spiritual Israel as they were currently being gathered up and brought back to the 'Land of Promise' established by covenant with Abraham.

Roma, a very special young man who loved the Lord and was always willing to help, became my faithful interpreter in the cell group and on other occasions as well. At times, I've seen the Lord perform His unique act of multiplication when it involves promotion of His Kingdom business. And so in this context, I later learned that the weekly teachings that the Lord had given me for the Jewish ministry cell group were being passed on by Roma to another Christian gathering that he was a part of. To my delight, my young Jewish interpreter, after attending a Bible school sponsored by one well-established international ministry in a city north of Portgarad, would eventually, along with his new wife, become the 'first fruits' of our cell group and congregation who would make the move to Israel. About five years after his departure from Russia, I would visit Roma, along with his wife and little boy in a city located south of Jerusalem. It was a joyful thing to see how the Lord was prospering them in Israel.

Many of those attending my cell group were not only bold and hungry for the Word of God, but they were determined to get the job done regarding God's plan for the Jews in our area. They would go after the Jewish colleagues that they worked with as well as friends and acquaintances that they knew to be Jewish. On a number of occasions, they would bring these men and women to me, setting up a meeting at a local park or elsewhere so that I could talk with them. Sometimes, I would be invited into the home of the Jewish friend or associate with full permission to share about aliyah and what the Word of God had to say about the Second Exodus from the mouths of the Old Testament prophets. When I felt the leading of the Lord, I would go ahead and share the Gospel as well, telling them about their Jewish Messiah. About once a month, our group sponsored 'shushlik' parties, (Russian/Ukrainian shish kabob), or tea and desert times when Jewish friends were invited to hear about aliyah, Israel, and the God of Abraham and His Son Yeshua, the Anointed One! These were great times for the Kingdom and for our excited cell group members as well because we got to see the Hand of God mightily at work among His people. The results of our labor did produce visible fruit, though the Lord Himself only knows the extent of it, because after all, it was His

Work and is credited to His glory alone! Our little band of zealous disciples merely constituted the willing vessels that were joyfully and obediently put to good use. But in the end, some of our Jewish friends were introduced to their Messiah, stirred up to consider aliyah, and reconnected back to their 'Jewishness' that had been nearly obliterated by seventy years of communism. There was even a report that one Jewish man we had prayed for, who was dying of cancer, had been supernaturally healed as well.

I have a great collection of stories from these events in Portgarad, like the time we were given permission to hand out literature and talk with theater goers as they attended a play put on by a visiting Moscow theater group comprised exclusively of Jewish Russian actors. The event was held at a very elegant and famous theater in Portgarad and was well attended by Jews in the area, not to mention visiting dignitaries who frequented this Soviet resort city. One such dignitary, a very high official in the Soviet government and second only to the top man of the political entity he served, gave his heart to Jesus after we had talked with him a second time during the week. Before he left Portgarad, he gave us his private phone number, instructing us to call him should any problems arise that he could help with. I'll never forget the warning that he specifically gave to me as an 'American'! I was told that there was a faction within the current Russian regime that was trying to gain control. If they succeeded, the United States would be in great danger. Since 'Perestroika', a false impression of a new and friendly Russia had been created for the benefit of the free world. But in reality, should this evil entity gain the upper hand and take control of the remnant of the old Soviet system, then there would be missiles and warheads aimed directly at America with the intention to strike! It was a sobering warning, but not a surprise to me. I recalled seeing hundreds of brand new tanks rolling by me on railway flat beds just months earlier when I had visited one remote location outside of Moscow. As I watched this display of wartime hardware, the Holy Spirit instructed me that the evil intent of the Communist empire hadn't really gone away as the media and the current world system wanted to make everyone think. It was merely wearing a new, more benevolent mask.

Yes, there were many such stories, like this one, that perhaps one day I will commit to paper. But for now, I need to move on. I mustn't forget to tell you about that marvelous blue and white ship symbolically decked in the colors of the Israeli flag. As my wonderful God had planned and promised, it eventually made its way to the Portgarad port, ready to carry many precious Jewish travelers who had been destined to fill its decks and chambers.

Chapter Fifteen

"The Ship Comes In!"

I'm not sure how long it was before news started surfacing about the ship, perhaps five or six months into my time in Portgarad. As I recall, our Russian congregation had received communication from the European ministry who was sponsoring the ship. Portgarad had indeed been the city chosen to host the ship and the aliyah ministry. What God had shown me months before was actually coming to pass. Little did I realize what my humble part was to be in all of this!

* * * * * * * * * * *

It was a snug fit, but we somehow managed to squeeze everyone inside my living room with an overflow group carefully listening from the adjoining porch. Most of our sprawling cell group was present and accounted for along with a few curious folks from our congregation. The occasion of this gathering was to host three representatives from the ministry that was sponsoring the boat. They had come to talk specifically to our Jewish ministry cell group to inform us about their mission and to seek out the right volunteer help for the upcoming operation. It was a high point indeed for the members of our group. They had been 'in training' since the cell group's inception, and like soldiers getting ready for a specific assignment, quite a few of them were eager to be launched out as helpers and volunteers.

Later in the week, a number from the Jewish ministry cell group filled out applications to become volunteers with the boat ministry. I was asked to make recommendations about each one before the volunteers were selected. Understandably, the ministry behind the boat was rather closed and guarded about their task and so they carefully scrutinized each potential helper. It was stated very clearly that there would be no 'evangelizing' of the Jewish brothers and sisters bound for Israel. To do so could jeopardize the existing cooperation between the Israeli agencies that were involved and this Christian organization. I'll admit that I questioned their approach at first, but the Lord compared the situation, for me, to a family that was being trapped in their house when it suddenly caught on fire. Certainly it was more important to first get the sleeping family members out of the house to a place of safety. Once they were brought into that place, then the God of their forefather, Abraham, could open their eyes to Yeshua their Messiah. In addition to this picture of the burning house, the Lord led me to several places in the prophetic Old Testament book of Ezekiel. Here it was written that the Jewish people would be spiritually awakened to know Messiah after they had been re-gathered to Israel.

"For I will take you from among the nations, gather you out of all countries, and bring you into your own land. Then I will sprinkle clean water on you, and you shall be clean; I will cleanse you from all of your filthiness and from all of your idols."(Ezekiel 36:24, 25)

FIRST they're brought back to their own land, and THEN they're made clean! Of course, that ultimate cleansing comes from being, "washed by the water of the Word",(Eph. 5:25), and Who is the Word? None other than Yeshua Himself, the Word made flesh, the Messiah!

Regarding the ship, my role turned out to be one of preparation…getting the folks ready to help! But as I realized later on, this too had significance in the Heavenly Kingdom as those from the cell group who were invited to help made up a significant part of the initial core of the boat ministry volunteers. Yes, among my tasks at Portgarad, God had used me to get them ready, passing on to them the love that God had instilled in my heart for the children of Israel. Even those in our group who had not been called on to perform specific tasks were asked to cook and deliver meals to the volunteers, the brothers who labored at such tasks as building wooden crates for the household items that would be carried to Israel. They worked very hard and needed to be fed. Also, the going away celebrations for our Jewish brothers and sisters who had traveled to Portgarad, as they got ready to embark the ship bound for their "Homeland", required baking and food preparation. I was pleased that the ladies in our cell group were more than willing to help, especially one lady named Masha who organized the cooking projects. A new and excited believer herself, Masha came to the Lord as a result of our cell group and eventually was promoted as a vital and trusted assistant to the European staff.

I must share, though, that I was disappointed about the polite, but obvious exclusion that I felt regarding any personal or direct involvement with the boat project. For example, I was never welcomed to go inside to see the facilities in the boat and how I longed to do that! I was content, though, to know that this European ministry was pleased that God had gotten the folks in this Russian charismatic congregation ready to help them with many of the practical aspects of the project. And so that was my assigned portion for this particular season. Later though, about five years into the future when the boat had stopped sailing from this port and was dry docked at some Mediterranean port, and when the European staff had been reassigned to another Russian city to coordinate airlifts to Israel, God sent me back into Portgarad. It was at this time that a special new assignment regarding the aliyah was made, one that the Lord would use me to initiate and help establish. The invaluable connections that had been made and the trust that was built during my year and a half stay in Portgarad would be vital to this future event.

A key figure in this aliyah ministry that God had raised up after the boat ministry was my dear Armenian friend Amari. As I mentioned in the last chapter, he and his wife, Vera, had established a thriving Bible school attached to the Russian church that had served as my spiritual covering. The Lord quickly knit our hearts together and we became very good friends despite the language and cultural barriers. Several times, I was asked to be a guest teacher in their school, and in fact was invited to become one of the regular staff for the following school year. I was really in my element when sharing the Word of God with these special Russian students who were so full of His Life! They were like sponges, ready to absorb and act on all that was taught. Though I had to teach through an interpreter, God's precious anointing on His vessel was preserved and very intense. I can honestly say that there is nothing in this earthly kingdom comparable to operating under the unction of God's anointing! And because the Words of God's Book were fresh and new to these Bible school students who were young believers, much ground had to be covered in a short amount of time. It took the intensity of His anointing to accomplish this.

Looking back, I was really in my spiritual heyday during my time in Portgarad. How I loved doing the works of my Father in this place! I really felt used and in tune with God's agenda and His timetable for me. At the end of 1995, I got ready to make a short trip to the States to visit with family and friends, planning only to be absent for about four weeks. I knew that I couldn't be away for very long because I needed to return in time to prepare for the new class of Bible School students. As I said good-bye to all those I had come to love in Portgarad, I didn't realize that my Heavenly Abba had different plans for me...only three and a half years later in 1999, I would eventually make my way back to this port city, but not before. It would be necessary to wait until it was God's season to open a brand new chapter. And when this happened, I would be sent out from Jerusalem, not some city in the United States. Little did I realize back then the surprises, and yes, the difficulties that lie just ahead!

Chapter Sixteen

"Florida & the Unexpected Assignment"

It had been about a year since I'd been in the States to visit with family and friends. My parents, who had moved from a cold, snowy New England state just five years earlier, had settled on Florida's west coast. There they built their two-bedroom retirement home in a quiet but growing community. It was a lovely home with a swimming pool, large enclosed porch, and a good-sized yard. But it seemed too small at times for the four of us. You see, my older sister Regina and I had taken on the responsibility of helping Dad care for our mother at home. Mom was slowly deteriorating away mentally with Alzheimer's disease, not to mention her poor physical condition following open-heart surgery a couple of years earlier. To top it all off, Dad had prostate cancer. It was a sad situation indeed that I encountered when I arrived home to visit from Portgarad! I knew deep down inside that I couldn't return to Russia. My God was grounding me at this juncture because I needed to be with my family. And so it grieved me and was difficult to face up to, but I knew that I couldn't go back! The situation was growing steadily worse and soon Regina wouldn't be able handle it alone. For the time being, she had to continue her job as RN with a home health care agency in a neighboring county and Dad needed more help with Mom. The picture of unfolding events didn't look very good. I agreed to stay on and take the bulk of the responsibility with Mom. But later, Mom's condition would lead to death and then Dad, suffering from a spreading cancer, would need extensive professional care. At that point, Regina quit her job to take care of Dad while I picked up a position as a medical social worker with one agency.

This very tough situation continued on for over two years, first loosing Mom and then about a year later, burying Dad. There are many sad memories that continue to linger from this time period. It's not easy to watch your parents waste away either physically or mentally. But as usual, the Holy Spirit was right there to help, sustain, and encourage despite Satan's blanket of death and gloom that he tried to suffocate with. I was, and continue to be, thankful to Jesus, the Son of the Living God of Abraham, Isaac and Jacob, because He already conquered sin and death and therefore death has no hold over those who are His. And though the battle for physical life was tragically and prematurely lost regarding my parents, one day I expect to see the dead raised to life! Here I must ask the question, "why not"? Just as it happened in the days of the Old Testament prophets and it happened in the days of Jesus the Anointed One, it can happen today!

One of the blessings that resulted from this time of serving Mom and Dad was that Regina and I got to be very close. We had always felt close as sisters, but somehow joining together to care for Mom and Dad on the home front caused us to become a united force, always watching out for the mental health and well being of each other. I can remember the "trapped in the house" feeling I experienced while trying to handle Mom. Regina always made sure that I got away for a little break, taking me out to supper or for a stroll through the mall. There were times when we couldn't leave the house for even a couple of hours, so a quick evening walk through the neighborhood had to suffice as a time to smell the sweet night jasmine, but also to vent and verbalize the frustrations and heartache of the day's activities. God seemed to give me special grace and patience to deal with Mom's Alzheimer's condition, while Regina had the medical qualifications to take care of Dad's needs. This team work and special relationship between Regina and I has carried over to this very day. If it were not for Regina keeping things going back in the States, it would be very difficult for me to be doing Abba's work here in Israel today where I currently sit writing this book. I like to tell her, every so often, that she has as big a part in what God is doing here in Israel as I do, and perhaps even more! Everyone needs to be so blessed to have a sister like Regina!

I don't want to linger too long on this chapter of my life other than to say that somehow I made it through those two years and was able to look ahead to some fresh new things that God had planned. When the family estate in Florida was finally legally squared away, Regina and I felt that we should pool together our portion of the inheritance money and buy a house in Tennessee. We both wanted 'out of Florida' and the local retirement community! My daughter Alice, who had attended college in this state, married her college sweet heart and resided in an area not too far from Nashville. Regina's daughter and son-in-law remained in Florida, but Regina and I felt that one day they, too, would make the trek to the hills of Tennessee.

The Lord quickly facilitated the purchase of a comfortable post World War II home with a lot of room and a big back yard. It was nestled in a small town between Nashville and Chattanooga. In many ways, our new home reminded us of the family house that we had grown up in except that our neighbors spoke with a southern drawl rather than a Yankee or French Canadian accent! We were able to pay for most of the house with only a small note pending, making it possible for Regina to keep up with some very modest house payments in my absence. This was all planned out ahead of time, of course, as both of us knew that at some point the Lord would be sending me out again. I must admit, though, that I didn't realize how quickly He would orchestrate such a change! My father passed away in August of 1997. By Christmas of the same year, Regina and I were fully settled into our new home. And by early spring, I was on an airplane bound for Israel! Some of the most exciting chapters of my walk with God were about to unfold. I was experiencing the Kingdom principle that on the other side of death, we can always find new life. God was about to raise me up, dust me off, and use me in a very unique way!

PART III

All Roads Lead To Jerusalem

Chapter Seventeen

"The Long Awaited Door Swings Open at Last!"

There are those times when the Lord will speak and His children must patiently wait until it's His season and moment to bring it to pass. Try as we may to cause it to happen beforehand, we cannot. But when we're actively about his daily business, faithfully tending to His directives, the season does eventually arrive when our spirits become quickened by the Holy Spirit, alerting us that a change is on the horizon. An excitement begins to stir from deep within us. The Words and Promises disclosed so long ago are injected with new life! We cautiously ask ourselves, could it be that God is about to do this thing at last?

This was the question I had found myself asking…

Regina and I were physically 'settled' in Tennessee, with my daughter, son-in-law, and grandbabies nearby, but somehow I couldn't get spiritually and emotionally settled. There was a kind of restlessness brewing within and I sensed that my plans to plug into some social service job and become a good friend and neighbor of the sleepy southern community I had moved into wasn't in the hand that God had just dealt me. The old desire to be in Israel started to haunt me. Surely God wouldn't move me on so quickly, I thought. Besides, I had barely broken in my beautiful bedroom furniture and how could such a move to Israel open up right now? My mind wandered to the practical…finances would be needed. I attended a tiny struggling church that lacked the means to support 'sent out' ones and besides that, I didn't have even the first connection with anyone in Israel! Yet, the Holy Spirit kept nudging me forward with the topic of Israel.

At last, I got brave enough to start verbalizing what I was sensing, even if it sounded impossible and far-fetched. After all, I reminded myself, my God majors in the impossible! I discussed going to Israel with my pastor and the man who was his spiritual covering at the time. They both encouraged me to test the waters further regarding Israel. There were no promises of missionary support, but that was okay with me as I sensed the Spirit of God advising me to steer clear of binding myself to any one particular group or Christian organization. Just having their blessing to go and encouragement would be enough.

As I learned later on, the spiritual covering that God had foreordained would appropriately come from the Israeli pastor and congregation in Jerusalem that the Lord was building me into. Had I operated under the direct spiritual covering of some church or Christian organization in the States, this would have been contrary to God's purposes for me. Also, from the onset, I knew that I wasn't being sent to help start some new church. Heaven knows that there is more than enough confusion in the States over endless church groups and denominations, not to mention second and third generation splinter groups derived from the mother church. It didn't take me long to figure out that Israel already had enough spiritual confusion to deal with! They didn't need the addition of assorted church plantings from the Nations. The God of Abraham, Isaac, and Jacob was more than able to raise up local shepherds and congregations from among the sheep in Israel, establishing congregations that were in keeping with the unique culture and experience of the Jewish nation.

The green light to move ahead with plans for Israel was definitely on. The next step was to pray about a connection with Israel. It wasn't long before the Lord showed me one. As it turned out, one lady in a nearby community 'just happened' to have visited the little church I was attending on the Sunday morning that Bro. George had 'just happened' to ask me to speak, sharing whatever the Lord put on my heart. This invitation to speak was all that I needed! Israel was brewing in my heart and mind and so I naturally felt led to teach and share about the sons and daughters of Jacob. I honestly don't remember exactly what the Holy Spirit led me to say, but I think that it had to do with the prophetic nature of the 'Second Exodus' of Jews returning to Israel in these current 'last days'. What I do remember, though, is that the anointing was very strong that morning and the Holy Spirit was stirring. A few weeks following all this, I learned from Bro. George that this lady, mentioned earlier, who had visited our congregation had a Jewish background. She and her husband ran a business in one remote, tucked away area in a neighboring county. Something inside of me clicked on as soon as the word JEWISH emerged from his mouth! I got the lady's phone number, explained that I was the one who had shared the message on the morning of her visit to Bro. George's church and we set up a time to get together.

Jean turned out to be not only Jewish, but Russian as well and a strong believer. She and her husband had spent time on the mission field themselves and were now serving the Lord with the business facility they ran. Jean told me that her husband, Danny, had a pilot's license and that one day they expected their facility would be used as a place of temporary refuge for American Jews en route to Israel. This of course would be a time of crisis in the U.S. when it would no longer be safe or comfortable for the Jewish population to remain. Their business facility had many acres of land, making it possible to build a small airfield to accommodate Danny's plane.

As Jean and I talked on, I shared my story about being in Russia and how God had spoken to me way back in 1985 about the second Exodus of Jews and involvement in the aliyah ministry. I continued to explain the strong unnatural, indeed 'supernatural' pull towards Israel that I had had since my youth. I told her that now was the time for Israel, and that I had felt led to seek her out sensing that she might be a connection! Jean appeared startled, excited, and somewhat touched by the emotions of the moment. "Why, yes, I do know one person who lives in Israel", she said, "she was a speaker at a Women's Aglow meeting some time back."

This lady that Jean referred to turned out to be my connection! I was so thankful that I followed the Holy Spirit's nudge, overcoming any shy or awkward feelings of going to a total stranger for the purpose of sharing my story and hoping to discover the next step in the implementation of God's plan. Herein lies yet another key, I believe, in God's supernatural leading. When the stirrings of the Spirit of God persist, we need to take some kind of action. There needs to be a response. It doesn't mean that you dive headfirst into unknown waters without an absolute 'green light' from the Holy Spirit, but it does mean that you're at least willing to stick your hand into the water to check the temperature and to proceed from there. This is obedience prompted by that first initial step of faith. If I hadn't followed the leading I was sensing from the Holy Spirit, I would never have met Jean and made the connection God had established for me. Without that piece of information, I may never have made it to Israel in the first place, making it impossible to participate in the multiple blessings that God had preordained for me there. I would have totally missed out on being Abba's catalyst to get a new aliyah ministry started and I would have lost the opportunity to have my life greatly impacted and transformed by one ministry located in the heart of God's fiery furnace, Jerusalem, and…

Jean adamantly tells me that it was only two weeks after our meeting that I was on a plane bound for Israel. For some reason I had thought that it was at least three! What I do recall very clearly, though, is that the Lord had instructed me that I was to go to Israel initially for a period of two to three months. During that time He would show me what city He would locate me in. After that, I was to go back to the States, get my things together, and return. In the process of settling in, further instructions would follow!

Chapter Eighteen

"The Honeymoon with Jerusalem Begins"

It was a long trip that brought me from Nashville to Chicago, and then to Frankfort and at last to Ben Gurion Airport in Tel Aviv. No one was there to greet me, but that was to be expected since I didn't know a soul from Israel anyway, save the Lord Himself, and it was He who had become my faithful traveling companion and ever-present Friend!

While I was in transit at the Frankfort, Germany airport during the wee hours of the morning, I encountered a group of ultra Orthodox Jews for the first time. The sight of them intrigued me and so I very carefully studied them from a distance. I noted that without exception the men were dressed in long black coats, trousers and round-brimmed hats. Under their hats they wore 'kippot', round black skullcaps that served to remind the world, which had so often rejected the sons of Abraham, of the existence of its Jewish citizens. The women also tended to dress in black and other dark colors, being well covered from head to toe with their long skirts, dresses or jumpers. I noticed that all of the married women wore hats and/or wigs to cover their natural tresses. And as I would learn later, some of the married women actually shaved their heads, denying the "crowning glory" that the Lord had given to them, exchanging their own hair for something stiff and unnatural! This was done to avoid any danger of violating religious law regarding any man, other than their husband, viewing their hair and becoming attracted to them! Yes, the whole scene was quite fascinating, and in some ways sobering for this newcomer who had never been exposed to an Orthodox Jewish community.

At a certain hour, the Jewish men congregated in the back corner of the large passenger waiting room, creating the effect of a patchwork sea of blacks and whites as they drew their large white and cream-colored prayer shawls over their heads and shoulders.

Wrapped in these, their holy garments, they separated themselves from the rest of the world as they swayed to and fro reciting the ancient prayers of their fathers from the well-worn pages of little prayer books. Hanging from each of the four corners of their prayer shawls was 'tsit tsit', the fringes that the Bible talks about in the Old Testament, (Numbers 15:37-41). Cited in the New Testament as well, I recalled the story about the woman with the issue of blood who touched the 'fringe' of Jesus' garment and was healed! It was actually the 'tsit tsit' of His prayer shawl that she had touched! I paused for a moment as I continued to watch these men, sadly realizing that they were unwilling to recognize Jesus, their Jewish Messiah, actually called Yeshua in the Hebrew tongue. I knew that they were destined to meet Him, though. The Word of God said so! And so I joyfully acknowledged that my appointed time in the Land would give me a front row seat to observe this future event! Yes, my God was good. Before long, the same airline that would be carrying these Jews back home to Israel would be bringing me 'home' as well. This was part of my inheritance and destiny, too, as Abba would later reveal to me. Just a few more hours and I would be stepping onto Israeli soil. Though my body felt sluggish with lack of sleep, my spirit was rejoicing. Just a little while and I'd be there.

My first impressions of Jerusalem and Ruth Benjamin, the lady who would be my hostess and apartment mate for the next two and a half months, were entertained as she greeted me in cautious fashion, poking her head out the back door entrance of her apartment and then quickly retreating back inside. I noted that she resided in an older and rather unappealing building that badly needed a facelift and some major repair work. It was located very close to the back entrance of the 'shuk', (a well-known outdoor market in Jerusalem), in the heart of one of the religious neighborhoods. I could almost immediately sense a spiritual oppression clinging to the area. It was not unlike the same feeling I had experienced at the airport while I observed the Jewish Orthodox there.

I knocked on the door a second time and at last got a verbal response. "Just one moment please," Ruth hastily exclaimed in familiar American English. I waited outside while she got herself together. I was feeling relieved that the taxi driver at the airport had delivered me safely to the correct Jerusalem address, but I wondered what my current living situation would be like. Finally I was invited to come inside. As Ruth sat in her stuffed chair wearing a polite smile on her face, I sensed that she was understandably keeping her guard up during our introduction. I studied her countenance and her person as well, all the while taking in the surroundings. Carved cherry furniture, a gift from friends in the United States, cheered up the dreary living room. Against the wall in a back room adjoining the living room, I could see a lovely upright piano, which, I was told, was also a gift. I was advised that this adjoining room would be mine. In it was a twin-sized bed standing opposite the piano. The bed was elegantly topped with a green silk bedspread. Lace curtains adorned most of the windows of the apartment, completing an air of aristocracy despite the humble appearance of the building itself.

Ruth seemed to me a little like her apartment in that she presented herself in the best possible light. A woman well into her middle years, she took great care to adorn herself in elegant long dresses and hats, giving the appearance more of someone from the royal courts, rather than from the stark streets of her neighborhood. Unfortunately, some misinterpreted the way that she dressed and carried herself as snobbery, but I came to understand and appreciate her as one of the King's special daughters. Why not display oneself as a person of value and worth? After all, we become what our words speak and our images project!

An unusual woman, as I would later learn, Ruth was a true survivor of the intensive spiritual battles going on over Jerusalem. Laced with a staunch determination to serve the Lord in Israel, she had maintained her presence there against great odds and

121

opposition. To help keep the needed finances flowing, she would take in visitors such as myself.

My first night in Ruth's apartment was laced with sleepless intervals, partly due to jetlag, but also because of my excitement. I could hardly believe that I was really in Jerusalem! What kind of spiritual adventures would await me, I thought? I nestled my head down into my pillow. Somehow the Presence of God seemed more intense and closer. The Holy Spirit reassured me that I could safely enter His rest and so I eventually nodded off for a few hours, falling into a deep sleep. When I finally awoke sometime in the morning, it took a little while to orient myself. No, I certainly wasn't back in my bedroom in Tennessee! I shook myself, evicting my body out of bed because I was anxious to begin exploring this most unique city. What awaited me that first day and the days that followed would prove to be both too wonderful to imagine, as well as an abrupt challenge to mature and grow in the things of the Kingdom. "Ruth", I politely inquired, "how do I get to the market from here?"

Chapter Nineteen

"Driven to My Prayer Closet!"

As the Holy Spirit had instructed me, I did indeed end up spending from two to three months in Israel initially, (actually two and a half months to be exact), and He did show me that my appointed place in Israel would be Jerusalem. As much as I felt drawn to the Russian Jewish believers in the North and could have easily settled in with one congregation there, I knew that that wasn't where I belonged. For some unknown reason, the Lord made it clear to me that I needed to be in Jerusalem. So I made a quick trip back to the States, packed my two rolling duffle bags as full as the airline weight limits for international travel would permit, and made my way back to God's Holy City. There, I continued sharing housing with Ruth, only this time upon my return it was in her new apartment that was located in a better area of town. The spacious bedroom she had set aside for me had high ceilings and large windows. It was more private, and thankfully so, because many hours would be spent in that room over the next five and a half months. There I would seek the God of my Fathers to learn what His Spirit would say to me. You see, I experienced an intense drawing during that time to press into the Presence of God. It was because I had been driven into the wilderness by the Holy Spirit for the purpose of emerging from that place months later, empowered to walk out the vision that the Lord would show me. I knew deep down inside that I was getting ready for something major and so, without exaggeration, half of my waking hours were spent in that room praying, worshipping and pouring over the Scriptures. As I did this, my relationship with the Lord took on new and deeper dimensions during those months. Because I desired to be tucked away with Him so much, I veered away from nearly all of the assorted Christian meetings and Messianic activities that flooded Jerusalem except for the congregation that the Lord had planted me in. There I faithfully attended, thankful to be led to a place where I could be truly fed and trained by the Word of God.

I have to admit that during this period of time, light conversation became burdensome to me. If what was being spoken was not focusing directly on the Lord and His doings, then I just wanted to be off by myself. Unfortunately, Ruth and others failed to fully understand my 'separating out'. I wasn't trying to be self-righteous, nor was I purposefully anti-social. The fact was that I was so hungry and thirsty for God that my hanging out on the mountain with Him took first place. Everyday socializing and relationships with people had of necessity to take a back seat, at least for awhile until I could get my relationship with the Lord and His priorities straight in my life.

And so it went for those five plus months, until one day the Holy Spirit clearly spoke to me giving me instructions to make a return trip to Portgarad. I reacted by being a bit startled at first, but excitedly welcomed and embraced His words. Many thoughts raced through my mind all at once, I remember, as I tried to understand the purpose and details of such a visit. Then some strong words followed...they came almost in the form of an admonition, "You're not to go alone!"

The Lord knew me well because up to this point most of my adventures and assignments from Him had been done 'Lone Ranger' style. My immediate response was, "Then who's supposed to go with me?" I realized that I had only been in Israel for less than six months and that close friendships in this place didn't come easily. Suddenly, the face of one sister in the fellowship I was attending flashed before me like a personality on a television screen. I really didn't know her, other than to smile or say 'hello' in passing. The reader can imagine her surprise when I announced to Christine where the Lord was sending me and who He had selected to accompany me! I can remember breaking this news to her in a small group that had gathered to pray. Saying almost nothing at first, she responded in dismay with a nervous kind of chuckle. I later learned that one of the two countries she had told the Lord she'd never want to go to was Russia! As it turned out, the One who had spoken to me began to speak to Christine's heart as well. In faith, I booked and paid for two airline tickets and the required entry visas, trusting God all the while for the finances. As usual, He was faithful to supply what was needed though it was a big step for me to believe, not only for myself, but for another person as well.

All of this occurred in 1999. The Lord first spoke to me in January directing me to make this initial visit back to Portgarad, but this was not the only trip that I would make to this city. Two other trips would follow that eventually led Christine and I to additional cities on the Black Sea coast as the groundwork was laid for an aliyah outreach to Jews in southern Russia. This, I learned, was God's purpose for sending me to Portgarad! By December of this same year, His work had miraculously spread into neighboring Georgia and Armenia. I continue to marvel at how God's plan unfolded during this year and how the Holy Spirit specifically directed and protected both of us as He sent Christine and me on these missions. I was amazed to see the Lord's hand supernaturally bringing together several Christian organizations in Israel and the States to sponsor the work. But the ultimate connection was with those precious Russian, Armenian, and Georgian believers who carried the mantle to do the work on site. Chief among them was Amari and his wife Vera, my beloved Armenian friends who had earlier founded the Bible school at Portgarad. Little did I know that this couple had moved on to plant a new church in Portgarad. This had happened during those interim years that I had spent in Florida as I joined my sister to care for our sick parents. Much to my dismay, it was this Armenian couple that the Lord told me to contact and stay with during that initial trip. Puzzled, I obeyed orders and made the connection, wondering why the Lord would not permit me to make contact with the large Russian church there that I had been so intimately connected to in 1994/95.

Sadly, the reason became clear soon after I arrived in Portgarad. Shortly after Amari met us at the airport, it was explained to me that some things had gone awry in this ministry, even to the extent of promoting false teaching regarding the prophetic directive of aliyah and the call for Jews to physically return to Israel. Crushed to learn that the leadership of this church had lost their clear vision for the work of aliyah, I was told that they now actually worked against it, taking the stance that Jews were supposed to get saved and remain inside Russia or their country of origin. Apparently one prominent Christian church in Moscow, (that I also had been familiar with earlier on), had been contaminated with this false teaching and was spreading it throughout Russia. I could see that the enemy was actively trying to destroy God's work. The seriousness of the matter was highlighted when, during my second trip to Portgarad, a group from this church in Moscow had arrived in Portgarad to teach a seminar that promoted this erroneous teaching. And guess who was hosting and sponsoring them? It was the large Russian church that had so warmly welcomed me five years earlier! I began to understand why the Lord had raised up a new church in this city. Not only that, but the aliyah boat ministry out of Portgarad had been suspended a couple of years earlier. There were still many Jews in this area who needed assistance to make aliyah. God had put it in the heart of this very special Armenian pastor and his Russian flock to do something about helping the Jews. They had been praying for God to somehow open the windows of heaven to use them in this very special ministry to the Jewish people. When the Holy Spirit had spoken to me in Jerusalem about going to Portgarad, little did I realize that I was being sent there in response to their prayers. God didn't need some famous evangelist or high-powered preacher to get the job done, just someone who was willing to obey and to act as His catalyst to bring all of the necessary people and resources together. As crazy as it all appeared in the natural, I was willing. I certainly wouldn't compare myself to Isaiah, but somehow I found myself in the Scriptures

where the Lord commissioned this prophet to 'go' and to carry out
a task, (Isaiah 6:8):

> *Also I heard the voice of the Lord saying:*
> *"Whom shall I send,*
> *And who will go for Us?"*
> *Then I said, "Here am I! Send me."*

Chapter Twenty

"Our Hearts Are Burning to Help the Jews"

It was the end of those first few weeks in Portgarad, an unforgettable time for me as I got to reunite with my Russian brothers and sisters that I hadn't seen for nearly five years. Actually, I had never expected to see them again this side of heaven, nor they me, but there they were wearing the accumulated victories and tragedies that had occurred in their lives since our earlier years together. I rejoiced to see how some had really matured and progressed in the things of God, while my spirit was saddened by several key young people who had been wounded and had lost their zeal for the Lord. Among them was the one I called my 'adopted' Russian daughter who was now in her early twenties. Because of her mother's problems, her grandmother was left with the responsibility of raising her, and so for some reason she clung to me, looking for the mother figure that she never had. As I greeted her that first Sunday after I arrived back in Portgarad, I couldn't help but notice that her countenance was hardened. Though polite and obviously wanting to see me, she seemed angry inside and distant. As I puzzled over her condition, a few days later I began to understand what was going on inside of her. The alarming story that had made the headlines, I was told, was that her natural mother now sat in jail somewhere in Russia. She had murdered a male friend and disposed of his body in a very gruesome fashion, the description of which made me shudder, (something that I'd rather not repeat here). As much as I wanted to go around and patch up this very sad situation and a few others as well, I knew that it was a tragedy that only the Lord could fix...

Many bouquets of flowers, little presents, hugs, joyful tears, and times of fellowship over 'chai' (tea) and Russian pastries welcomed me throughout the entire visit as I talked with this dear friend and that one. My limited Russian was pretty rusty at this point, but somehow we managed to communicate. What a blessing

129

it was to reconnect with these precious brothers and sisters! Yet I keenly sensed, via the Holy Spirit within me, that the main focus of the trip had to do with my favorite Armenian couple, Pastor Amari and his wife Vera, and so Christine and I spent much of our time visiting and praying with them. We also attended all of the prayer meetings, Sunday services and home cells groups connected with their newly evolving church that by now was about two years old. Yes, the days busily and pleasantly passed until, when midway through the visit, one sentence spoken in broken English emerged from Amari's mouth. His words caught me off guard, while at the same time they became etched within the deepest parts of me as he spoke. I knew that God was getting my attention and that these words contained the key to the Divine purpose for this visit. Amari's eyes were intense and focused as he sought to disclose the true yearning of the sheep in his congregation. "Our hearts are burning to help the Jews!" Something cut through my inner being like a knife. Amari went on to explain how the people had been earnestly praying for God to make a way for them to reach out to the many Jews in their area with both practical and financial services so that they could make aliyah and return 'Home' to Israel. One lady, he said, was willing to take on an additional job selling cosmetics hoping that God would prosper her so that she could give all of the money to help with aliyah. I had met this woman, a single mother who was left with the task of supporting and raising her own children on the meager wages she earned as a secretary. Yet she was willing to take on additional work to aid the children of Jacob! As the Lord showed me her heart and the sincere hearts of many in Pastor Amari's church, I wanted to weep. Only God could have put such a love for the Jewish people in the hearts of these Russian Christians, many of them only a few years old in the Lord. Christine was also noticeably moved and impacted by Amari's disclosure. We decided to spend the next few days really seeking God and praying about the matter.

It was just a day or two before our scheduled departure back to Israel that the four of us, Amari, Vera, Christine and I, were sitting in Amari's study room. I turned to my dear Armenian brother and pointedly addressed the subject of aliyah with a question, "What kind of help do you feel the Lord is equipping you to offer?" There was silence for a brief moment while Amari caught his breath, and then he dove in. That's almost all I got to say for the next couple of hours as he unfolded a progressive and complex plan to open an aliyah office in Portgarad. First there would be services to help the Jews with information about the process of being approved for aliyah under the 'Jewish Law of Return'. This meant not only directing them to Jewish Agency officials and places where various legal documents verifying that they or a parent, (or grandparent), were Jewish, but it meant financing trips to various cities where family birth and death certificates might be located. Then for many, a trip to Moscow would have to be financed so that they could get visas and passport documents authorizing them to enter Israel. Amari projected that at some point, the Lord willing, small planes could be chartered to airlift new immigrants from the Portgarad airport. He had even started estimating expenses for such a venture. Then there was the need to respond with practical assistance like helping to get luggage and personal belongings from point 'A' to point 'B'... Amari continued on with his well thought-out plan that extended far beyond the local region. By the end of his discourse, I 'knew that I knew' the Holy Spirit was asking me to do something to enable this vision to take on flesh. I was aware that Amari had many connections in the area and even favor with the local Jewish agency. This was a real plus! He knew the ropes when it came to aliyah, because before starting the church he now pastored, he had worked on the ship with the European minstry that had once transported new 'olim' to Israel from the Portgarad port. I knew this brother and I knew his heart. He was solid in his faith and not the kind of man who would give up in the middle of things when the going got rough. He and his congregation had counted the cost and were willing to see it through. Yes, as I pondered my own thoughts they seemed to intersect with my Heavenly Father's thoughts on the matter. As wild as it seemed, something had to be done to help. That's why I had been sent there, and that's why Christine had been commissioned to join me.

As if the Lord needed to stir my emotions any further, our departure flight from Portgarad had a number of families on it who were making aliyah. The familiar 'Russian' suitcases, that is, the large, white, square and zippered, woven nylon bags with black and red threads were sitting everywhere on the concrete floor. As many precious items as possible were stuffed into these bags and any other boxes, trunks or containers that could be found. It wasn't Samsonite luggage or businessmen traveling in three piece suits that I was looking at, but instead the struggling workers of old mother Russia who sought to plant their feet, their hopes, and their future generations in a familiar, but strange land, 'Yisrael'! The tears, the clinging embraces, and the good-byes between friends and family members stirred my heart as well. This wasn't just a scene out of a movie or a dream. Somehow I was also a very real part of it.

Christine and I boarded the plane clutching the cardboard boxes, secured with twine that contained the new Russian tea sets we had had a few moments to go out and purchase. I need to explain here that my original tea set had been left behind back in 1995, along with almost everything else, when God grounded me in Florida to care for my parents. Next to my Russian Bible, that was the item I missed the most as it represented all of those special times of fellowship with my dear Russian family. In fact, one young American who had been in Portgarad blessed me some months later by taking the tea set back to the States with him and then mailed it to me through the U.S. post. Unfortunately though, many of the pieces were broken. I remember crying, both with joy and with sadness, as I opened the mailed parcel and discovered the broken pieces. Trying to salvage a few of the cups, saucers, and dessert plates, I pulled out a tube of glue. But amazingly, the sugar bowl and creamer were in tact and the teapot itself was only damaged a little bit. And so this opportunity some five years later to come back with a new Russian tea set was very special to me. In my mind, I wasn't about to part with it, but Abba had other plans as I would later learn...

Chapter Twenty-One

"Riding on the Waves of a Miracle!"

Incredible and supernatural are the only words I can come up with to describe the days that followed that first trip into Portgarad! Amazingly, the Lord had spoken to two men in Jerusalem, both heads of organizations that either financed or orchestrated the works of aliyah in the field, and then set-up divine appointments with both of them. Christine was the connection to one of these brothers and I was led to come into contact with the second. In the end, an even more significant miracle occurred in that the partner organizations that these two men were connected with also became a part of our sponsoring team creating a first-time alliance between four well-established Christian groups. Joining hands to finance and provide the system and manpower to get the job done and to equip the local people to carry out the work of aliyah, these groups covenanted together to work as one to back up and support the work of aliyah out of southern Russia. Later on, Georgia and Armenia would be added to this precious work, something that the Holy Spirit had revealed separately to me and to one of the brothers. Regarding my part, it was understood from the beginning that I would move with the vision that the Lord was giving me. The resources that were needed to set up the aliyah work in Portgarad would be made available. The only stipulation was that accurate record keeping and reporting would be required in order to show that the monies were being properly spent. Christine and I were ecstatic!

Listening closely to the Voice of the Lord, I was given the dates to go back into Portgarad. When I contacted Amari to tell him about our miracle and pending return trip, he too was overjoyed and couldn't wait to get started. It wasn't long before Christine and I were back on a plane headed for some new adventures that not only blessed the future olim out of this area of the world, but also tested most of us in the process. Personally, I was put through some heavy-duty fire, while all the while I had to stay balanced and settled in what God was doing. It would have been easy to fall apart and to respond in the flesh to some things that were going on, but I knew that I had to be the Lord's rock, so to speak, in this situation. I knew also that Amari recognized his most significant role as leader, stabilizer, and spearhead in getting the work established. In fact, I understood that not only would his responsibilities be ongoing, but that they were even weightier than mine. When my part in walking out the vision from the Jerusalem end would come to a close, Amari's part as visionary and leader in actually carrying out the work would continue. The enemy, of course, was not happy with any of us and worked overtime to bring division, using any weakness that he could find among those who had been called to be a part of the work. But this story is not so much about the struggles and testings of the enemy, as it is about the victories and advances made for the Kingdom of God. There were many! And so to continue...

This second trip lasted for six weeks. From beginning to end, we were amazed to see how the hand of God put everything into place. We were able to rent, set up, and equip an office with the basics, a feat in itself considering the Russian bureaucratic red tape that existed. Staff was appointed and shown what to do. Some would be responsible to receive clients and maintain records in the Portgarad office, while others would travel to cities and areas in the region. During those weeks, major connections were made with a couple of the Jewish Agencies. We gained great favor with one such agency located in a city, one day's journey by car, up on the Black Sea coast. I'll never forget our initial trip there as the agency director, a lady in her mid 50's or early 60's invited us into her office. A Jew herself, she had been trying her best with such limited resources to help the local Jewry, many of them living in desperate and impoverished situations, to get their papers together to make aliyah. One kindly Jewish doctor, living on a shoestring, volunteered his time to help her with the work. He too sat in on that first meeting. Amari, Vera, Christine and I listened with our hearts as we were told some of the stories about the people this agency served, but the one that impacted me the most was the family that had migrated to this city from another area, hoping to get help with their aliyah. The teenage daughter from this family appeared on the agency doorstep during the time of our visit. I was told that the family was totally out of food and didn't know where to turn. Praise God, though we weren't prepared to actually start dispersing money yet, I had some rubles in my pocket that I could give them. It wasn't very much, but to them it meant being able to buy a few weeks groceries. What really broke me was the report I received later on that the young girl had been praying that God would somehow send them food. The Lord had permitted us to play a real part in the answer to her prayer! Nothing in the world can measure up to the joy one gets when you become a part of the Father's hand of blessing in these kinds of situations. There were many such stories as this, but I feel led to move on and share a different kind of story with the reader, another miracle event that took place during this brief six-week interval. This miracle event came in the form of a little Jewish baby boy named Michael.

Michael resided in the local Portgarad orphanage along with many other babies and toddlers who had been abandoned, given up, or bereaved of natural parents. I was told that the times had become so desperate for many, that the orphanage was not only full, but operating beyond its capacity to supply even the most basic needs of these precious little ones. Peering through the fence that enclosed the main building and the surrounding grounds, the four of us stood there trying to view the activity inside. I need to explain here that one didn't just ring the bell and enter, but had to get special permission. This was usually best achieved by finding an 'inside' connection! Well, our good God was faithful to hook us up with a local Christian lady who worked there. Upon our request, she was able, unofficially of course, to advise us that one little Jewish orphan resided in the Portgarad orphanage. You see, that was the ultimate focus of our visit. Other inquiries were made as

137

well into other orphanages in this region. The task at hand was to locate any Jewish orphans that may have existed and to get them out and into the hands of Jewish or Christian parents who would one day encourage their return trip home to Israel. I had been told that many such orphans existed in the Ukraine, but our investigation in this particular region, as limited as it probably was, only turned up one such child during this time.

One of the nannies came to the gate and opened it to let us in. The grounds were pleasant enough, I noted, as I watched some of the little ones taking in the warm summer air from carriages or from the laps of nurses and volunteers. Over to the side I spotted a clothesline full of freshly washed baby diapers. But there was something different about the way these diapers were hanging. Upon further investigation, I realized that what I was looking at were actually paper diapers that had been rinsed and hung out to dry for future use! It was later explained to me that cloth diapers were hard to get and that it was necessary to re-use the paper ones that they had. There simply wasn't sufficient money to buy more diapers. I silently groaned a little bit when I heard this, but was later comforted by the fact that at least everyone there seemed to be doing their best to care for the babies and young children. As I went inside the main building, I could see that it was kept very clean and orderly and the surroundings, though sparsely equipped, were pleasant. Being told that the director was not in that day but that we could make an appointment to talk with her in the future, we were content to tour the facilities and to observe some of the children. A number of the babies were sickly and clearly were not thriving. We were told that the children usually entered the orphanage in such a condition. The staff and volunteers did their best to nurse them back to health, but for the most part there just didn't seem to be enough hands or money to go around to meet the overwhelming needs of these precious little ones who had been through so much.

At the end of our tour, our guide motioned to us to sit down in an area off to the side. The lady who was our Christian connection with the orphanage scurried off into an adjoining room, returning a few moments later with a little lively bundle of energy in her arms. Four to six months old, it was so hard to tell, the little boy baby that she held had curly strawberry-blond hair and something built inside of him that many of the children seemed to lack, the motivation to press through and live! It's hard to describe this here, but it was something that I keenly sensed even in such a young child. I glanced over at Vera who was nearly mesmerized by the child. An almost incomprehensible delight flashed across her face as this childless woman, who was well into her 30's by now, picked up the baby boy. Amari looked on with great interest noting first his wife's special pleasure, and then taking stock of his own drawing to the little guy. This was Michael, the little Jewish baby who would a year or so later complete their family once the insurmountable Russian red tape was cut through. The process would require working with the authorities to get Russian passports for Vera and Amari, and in some cases, there would be gifts given, (the proverbial 'greasing of hands'), to those who had the power to aid or prevent the adoption of little Michael. Perhaps it wasn't the most ethical thing to do and foreign to the culture I grew up in, but it was the way of the old Soviet system and necessary to spring little Michael from the orphanage.

What else is there to say about this second trip? There was the most tedious journey I had ever taken in my life, going by car to one coastal city, on the bumpiest and longest road I had ever traveled! Our little caravan of cars from Amari's church traveled no less than 12 or 14 hours for this return trip back to Portgarad. The frequent delays were due to one of the cars in our group repeatedly breaking down along the way. We also had gotten off to a late start that day because one of the other cars had had a battery and some other car parts ripped off and stolen from it. That particular trip and mission was further highlighted in my mind after I had been attacked and bitten by a huge mongrel dog just prior to our departure! During this season following Perestroika in Russia, there was a real shortage of medical supplies and so injection needles were frequently re-used. I decided that I was better off not to get a rabies shot at this juncture, even if such a thing could be located. Fortunately though, Christine had some alcohol wipes in her purse. These would have to suffice, I decided, as I went back into the house of our host, closing the door to the bathroom behind me as I carefully cleansed the area of the dog bite located on my outer thigh. After it was all over with, I nearly fainted from a combination of fatigue, heat, and obviously from the trauma of being attacked. It was clear to me that the enemy was registering his vote of disapproval because God's work regarding aliyah and the Gospel was going forward. Still, I was thankful that I was the one who got attacked rather than Christine who came out of the house right behind me. As difficult as the trip had been for me, the supposedly 'seasoned' Russian missionary, it was even harder for her. Such an event as being the recipient of a dog bite could have understandably proved to be almost too much. We were all relieved to eventually make it back to Portgarad. Just a few short days later, Christine and I flew back to Jerusalem to prepare for the next phase of the aliyah work.

Chapter Twenty-Two

"Georgia, Armenia & Joseph Stalin's Boxcar"

A few weeks before booking plane tickets for our third trip, we received a disturbing e-mail from Amari. Actually, true to his nature, he tried to downplay the whole thing while at the same time he clearly wanted to alert us. Apparently right after Christine and I had left Portgarad at the end of our second visit, some KGB agents showed up asking questions about the American women who had been there. After hearing this news, I was thankful that this next trip would circumvent Portgarad altogether as the Lord had clearly laid it on my heart, the hearts of our sponsors, and on Amari's heart as well, that the aliyah work needed to spill over into neighboring Georgia and Armenia.

****

Early November, 1999, Tbilisi, Georgia:

Amari took a short flight from Portgarad so that he could meet us at the Tbilisi airport. Unprepared for the bone-chilling cold we found in Georgia, I clutched my lightweight jacket and pulled it tightly against me hoping to maintain whatever body heat I still had left. Struggling to forget how cold I was, I focused my thoughts on this leg of our supernatural journey. And supernatural it was! I pinched myself to make sure that all of this was real. Only the hand of our Mighty God could orchestrate and fine-tune the events that were rapidly unfolding before us. In less than six months, the work out of the Portgarad office in Southern Russia itself had spread to a number of cities both inland and on the Black Sea coast. Now during this third trip, we were looking at quite a sizeable number of Jews who lived in Georgia, many of them scattered in the villages and foothills. It would be both a blessing and a worthy challenge to send 'fishers' out to them to encourage and assist them to return to Israel. Additionally, this current trip would also focus on Armenia where there were at least a thousand

Jews remaining who had nearly been forgotten, even by the Israeli government. These Jews were the remnant of a large aliyah that had occurred some years back during a very troubled period in Armenia's history. And so, even now as I write this chapter of my book, I continue to marvel at the Divine groundwork that was laid to assist the Jews in both of these countries. It was during this trip that we met one of Amari's heaven-sent, and I must add, very colorful connections, a well-known and influential apostle from Amari's native Armenia. Part way through the trip the four of us were scheduled to come together during a hastily arranged supper meeting.

I think that I have enough stories and interesting descriptions from this trip alone to fill the pages of a modest-sized book, but for my purposes here will taper the story down to share only the highlights with you the reader. So to begin, our first few days in Georgia were spent meeting a couple of pastors, one from the Tbilisi area and the other from a city called Gori, located a few hours away by car from the Georgian capital. Both pastors shared that their congregations were willing and anxious to begin aliyah work in their respective areas. They would gladly hook up with the Portgarad office and take their direction from there. I recognized that like Amari and so many other Christian leaders and adherents to the faith that I had met in the old USSR, these two men had a real heart for the Jews and aliyah. It was a supernatural preparation of the heart that only God could do. Though I was impressed by both of these pastors and their willingness to be used in this precious work of God, I was especially drawn to the pastor from Gori. This young man had an angel's face; that's the only way I can describe it. He was so full of the Holy Spirit that there was a constant glow about him, even as he carried out God's work in the face of some hard and trying times in Georgia. I didn't totally understand the politics behind it all, but interference with the petroleum and fuel supplies, (From Mother Russia?), had created some very difficult living conditions for most of the Georgian population, especially during the winter months. In practical terms, it meant no electricity, heat, or hot water for most of the day. Even the cold water supply was turned off most of the time. So, to make sure that there was some water to draw from during the day, people would fill up their bathtubs with water in the wee hours of the morning during the brief interval that this vital utility was turned on. Still, despite these living conditions and other hardships, our pastor from Gori, along with the members of his family and congregation that we had met, continued to smile the most radiant smiles and to worship and praise God for His goodness.

Now I must share with the reader a little more about this city called Gori because it was the birthplace of Joseph Stalin who was one of the worlds most notorious and brutal figures who rose to prominence during the mid 1930's until his death in 1953. A contemporary and disciple of Vladimir Lenin, (taking over after Lenin's death), Stalin was a perpetrator of the Russian Revolution, and a sympathizer of the Nazi Anti-Semitic ideology that was sweeping through Europe. Stalin's policies laid the groundwork for the death of millions during his reign in the USSR. The gulags, forced labor camps that flourished during his rise to power, became death camps for many. Political prisoners, dissidents, undesirables, and those who were earmarked as enemies of the new Soviet regime were either exterminated outright or assigned to the gulags. This Soviet style Holocaust included countless Jews!

****

Recounting Stalin's incredibly evil role during this turbulent time in history, I shuddered from the icy cold that seemed to cling to the stone walls and floor of the Joseph Stalin museum in Gori. It wasn't just the physical cold I felt though, but the chilling eulogy of books, pictures, old letters and documents, furniture and assorted remembrances that comprised the trappings of this massive two-story stone and marble structure. Our angel-faced pastor who had brought Amari, Christine, and I to visit this famous site in his home town, stepped aside while the curator, a lady who

143

appeared to be in her late 60s or early 70s, recounted the stories and descriptions of the various museum pieces in Russian. Amari did his best to translate into English for us. I think that the most gruesome item we viewed was a death mask of Stalin. It was conspicuously encased under a large glass dome that filled the center of one enormous room in the museum. The lights in the room itself were turned down low while an eerie rose-colored glow from lighting within the case was projected upon the mask itself. Though one part of me curiously took in all of this with great interest, the other part of me couldn't wait for the tour of the museum, with its bone-chilling cold and lingering demonic presence, to end.

Once outside, all of us breathed a sigh of relief as we were ushered to two other structures on the museum grounds. The first was a small and very primitive wooden house that Joseph Stalin was reportedly born in. This was not terribly impressive I have to admit, and in fact I didn't really get to see much of anything inside as visitors were only allowed to peer into the main room of the building through a couple of small, cloudy, glass-pained windows. But the next structure that we approached definitely captured the interest of all. It was Joseph Stalin's personal boxcar that he and his companions traveled in during those terrible years of terror. If this boxcar could talk what stories would it tell, I thought! We were invited to step inside. There were two main compartments as I recall, the biggest one containing his personal seat. As each one of us took turns sitting in Stalin's chair, the heaviness of his horrendous deeds and presence was apparent. At the same time, sitting on the dictator's throne was a bold and victorious statement that symbolized, at least for me, Divine retribution and judgment for the evil done to so many. Soon many Jews from this very area of the world would be coming home to Israel just like the Almighty had promised in His Word! Yes, I mused, the very act of sitting in Joseph Stalin's chair was symbolically crushing the head of the enemy and claiming victory for the Kingdom of God and for all of the Jewish brethren.

144

The camera clicked as each of us was seated. I marveled that the birthplace of the one who had snuffed out so many Jewish lives, and others, would now become the birthplace for a new aliyah station. Many Jews seeking a new life in Israel would be helped and encouraged on their way by this pastor and fellowship of Christian believers in Gori. Prophetically, God had ordained all of this from the foundation of the world and here I was right in the middle of it! All the gold in Fort Knox couldn't buy a moment such as this. Had nothing else of significance happened during our trip, this would have been enough, but then I can't forget to mention our visit to one of the Jewish agencies in Armenia.

****

Crossing over from Georgia into Armenia by van would be a matter of immense prayer and endurance: prayer to make sure we'd be allowed through, and physical endurance because the roads were little more than beaten down, rutted paths in many places. Desperate Georgian policemen who hadn't received a salary for months and angry mixed-up youths hung out at various intervals of the roadway threatening to arrest the innocent travelers as "traffic violators" or to beat the van windows in with poles and wooden sticks unless their 'palms were greased'. The whole scene was quite disconcerting to say the least, but what could one do but pay the required bribe and pass on until the next human obstacle appeared. I actually felt bad for the police officers. They too had become victims in this system of corruption that had taken its toll on most of the population. Everyone seemed to have his hand out looking for money before safe passage would be permitted. And then there was one actual border crossing between Georgia and Armenia that we only got to go through by the grace of God and one good-hearted guard who bent the rules for us. Apparently, Christine and I didn't have the right stamps in our passports to be allowed through this particular crossing. And unbeknownst to our van driver, the rules had been recently changed about crossing at

145

this particular point. Had the issue not been resolved, we would have been left out in the middle of no man's land without transportation as our van driver had to continue on to his destination with the other regular passengers who were authorized to pass through.

Yerevan, Armenia:

The trials and tribulations that emerged from our travels were softened by the protection and Divine favor of the Almighty. We arrived tired and cold from Georgia, but safe at last in Yerevan, Armenia's capitol. Amari and his wife, Vera, had not sold their apartment in Armenia when they made their move to minister in Portgarad, Russia, and so while they retired separately to their own private quarters, Christine and I were escorted by our driver to an apartment belonging to Yevgeni's church. (Yevgeni was the apostle that we would meet later in the evening to discuss the aliyah work in his region. And as it turned out, the next day we would go to the Jewish agency in Yerevan to distribute money and lend assistance in any way that we could.) But in the meantime, God was literally shining His warmth and goodness on us by providing this wonderfully warm place to sleep and rest a little. You can't imagine how thankful the two weary travelers from Jerusalem were for this, but especially yours truly because of my tendency to get cold so easily! I can't remember ever being so miserable. I had been frozen to the bone since I had left Jerusalem especially while in Georgia where Christine and I had spent several nights with one family who huddled over a little homemade metal stove in the kitchen to stay warm. Carefully rationing out their meager supply of hazelnut shells to be fed into the fire, this family had no other source of heat for their apartment. At nighttime, Christine and I had to bury ourselves under piles of blankets in an attempt to get warm enough to fall asleep. After a few days of this, I honestly thought that my body was going into hypothermia. And so you can imagine the absolute delight that awaited us in this little apartment in Yerevan that had not only two electric heaters, but the electricity to run them as well! In the corner of the large main

146

room, two twin-sized beds with fluffy down covers and crisp white sheets beckoned us. And hallelujah to Jehovah Jireh, our God who supplies all of our needs, there was hot water for showers if one took them early enough in the morning! On the table we spotted a big luscious looking spread of fresh fruits, breads, cheese and nuts. It was almost like being in heaven!

That evening the young man who was our apostle's Timothy wasted no time driving us through the streets of Yerevan. As we drove to our appointment with Apostle Yevgeni, Christine and I learned about the network of churches that he had established in both Armenia and neighboring Georgia. Because of his work for the Kingdom, this man of God was greatly respected and recognized by the church leadership in both of these countries as well as in nearby Russia and the Ukraine. We were told that because of the authority that the Lord had given him, his word could either make or break a situation. Yevgeni's apostolic standing among his own became even more obvious as we watched Amari's usual easy-going and confident nature stand to attention the moment Yevgeni entered the local pizza restaurant we were meeting at. I must say that the whole scene was much more relaxed for Christine and me and in some ways it was even a bit humorous, especially when we saw our apostle approach our table clad in a black baseball cap and Nike running shoes! Yevgeni took a seat next to Amari and across from Christine and I. Looking more like a jogger or someone who was emerging from a workout at an American country club, he greeted us with a playful smile as I tried to put the whole scene together in my mind. In the meantime, our dear Amari clicked into a kind of "yes sir" mode as he began to translate from his native Armenian into English for Christine and me. Amari obviously had great respect for Yevgeni and so Christine and I were both delightfully amazed and thankful for this Divine connection that God had provided via Amari.

After ordering our pizza, the conversation opened with Yevgeni telling us how he had prayed, asking the Lord for direction before our meeting that evening. While in prayer, the Holy Spirit instructed him to do all that he could to further the aliyah assistance to the Jews in his region of the world. Regarding the work that had begun in Portgarad spreading into Georgia and Armenia, the Spirit of God had specifically said, "No obstacles and no boundaries!" Yevgeni continued on with a personal word for Christine and I, saying that everywhere we went an angelic host would go ahead of us to prepare the way. Though there were some tough and tense moments during our travels, especially as we crossed the border back and forth between Georgia and Armenia, we knew that these words were true. God was ever faithful to both guide and protect us and to make all the pieces of His perfect plan fall into place.

Christine and I returned to our cozy warm apartment after the supper meeting with Yevgeni. The following morning there was a knock at the door. It was Amari and Vera who had come to pick us up so that the four of us could make our scheduled visit to the Jewish Agency in town. The day ahead would be long and difficult for all, but perhaps even more so for Amari and Vera. They were the ones who would have to shoulder the responsibility for communicating with the agency director and the heads of ten or twelve families who were waiting for our assistance. Using my limited Russian, I was able to assist Amari and Vera somewhat and to chat with our precious clients who spoke both Armenian and Russian, but for Christine, I could see that the situation had become a bit frustrating due to the language barrier. Still, we all just kept on going, taking down information and trying to do our best for each family. I knew that Christine and I were scheduled to leave the following day so that we could get back to the airport in Tbilisi. But Amari and Vera had made arrangements to stay on in Yerevan for a couple days longer so that they could continue to process as many applications as possible. If the money on hand ran out, (and we knew that it surely would because the need was so great), then at least the sponsors could be contacted later on with these additional applications for assistance that Amari and Vera would process.

The hardships and obstacles that these remaining Armenian Jews had to face in order to get visa stamps and papers to immigrate to Israel were phenomenal. First of all, there was incredible red tape with the Israeli government itself who required them to travel all the way to Moscow to get proper authorization. This took, on the average, not one trip but two! And getting into Moscow meant going first to the Tbilisi, Georgia airport to catch a flight into Moscow where there was an Israeli Embassy. The journey to the Tbilisi airport from Yerevan was no piece of cake. Like all travelers, bribes would be taken on the roadways and at the border crossing into Georgia. Once at the Georgian airport, corrupt officials would be looking for special bribe money from their Jewish Armenian neighbors. To add to all of this, Armenia, with its own brand of corruption and broken down government, had a severe shortage of men who were army age. This meant that any Armenian Jewish man who wanted to immigrate to Israel was required to pay substantial bribes to the tune of $1000 to $1500 to Armenian army officials! The younger the potential soldier was the higher the bribe. Men up to the age of about fifty were victimized by this practice. We heard from one family in Yerevan that a $3000 bribe was required before the army would release their son to make aliyah. That first day at the Jewish Agency we all left with heavy spirits and frustration after learning that such things were going on. Not only did it make it almost impossible for some of these Jewish men to leave Armenia, but many families would have to depart for Israel without sons, brothers, or fathers, until some miracle could be worked out later on. Living conditions for these remaining thousand or so Armenian Jews were worse than for the general population it seemed. But the Azerbaijanian Jews, who had fled across the borders into Armenia, experienced even worse conditions. One of these Azerbaijanian families met us at the Jewish agency in Yerevan. They had such an entangled web of physical and medical needs, (not to mention the additional hoops that they would have to jump through to get their papers processed and authorized), that we knew only a miracle of God would release them out of their Egypt and into the Land of Milk and Honey.

****

Back in Tbilisi:

As I said earlier, this chapter could easily become a book in itself. But let me end it here with one last rather humorous note. It was while Christine and I were traveling by car one morning through the streets of Tbilisi, that Artur, our sweet, kind, (and I must add quick-witted), driver, suddenly barreled up and around onto one of the sidewalks. His foot on the gas, he sped through the thick crowds of Georgians who had come out to see the Pope during his special Papal visit to their country's capitol. This event just happened to coincide with our current aliyah mission trip. Eventually our vehicle landed back safely onto the more familiar black road pavement. Apparently while watching one delegation of European officials press through the blocked streets, having been granted special permission to pass by the Georgian militia, Artur our driver decided to make a similar maneuver as he called out in his native tongue, "The American delegation...the American delegation, we're coming through." And through the thick crowds we surely went! Christine and I laughed with delight as soon as we had realized what Artur had done. Perhaps it wasn't the 'Popemobile', and we certainly didn't count ourselves among the dignitaries or important personages of any group, yet deep down inside we realized that we were there 'for a time such as this' to represent our King, Yeshua, and His heavenly Kingdom on behalf of the Jewish Diaspora in this country.

Back to Jerusalem, the Amazing Trip Ends:

As Christine and I got in line at the Tbilisi airport to board our plane back to Jerusalem, Artur waited to see us off. Handing each of us a brightly wrapped rectangular package, he beckoned us to open it. I pulled off the paper first and carefully read about the

150

contents, 'Petichka Moloko', I excitedly informed Christine, 'Bird's Milk!' I went on to explain that it was a special kind of chocolate-covered candy that I had eaten many times before in Russia. Then I sadly paused for a moment knowing that the journey for now had ended and that the 'American delegation' might never see dear Artur again this side of heaven. Christine and I exchanged both hugs and tears with our precious Georgian brother who had given so freely of his time and the use of his private vehicle. And then it was time to go.

As our little plane began to lift itself off from the Tbilisi airport runway, I quickly reviewed the events of this current trip and thought about what Heaven might have next on its agenda. Surely there would need to be at least a couple more trips back into Portgarad to get everything settled and in place, especially with the new doors that God had just miraculously opened in Georgia and Armenia. And then after that Christine and I would be able to keep track of all the aliyah record keeping, etc., by e-mail. Perhaps money could somehow get into Amari's hands for distribution by wire transfer rather than having to hand-carry it as we had done during these past three trips. I knew in my heart that at some point Christine and I would be phased out and that the trust that I had established with Amari years ago in Portgarad could be safely transferred to our network of sponsors in America and Jerusalem. I was prepared and truly willing for this transfer and phasing out to happen in God's timing! But, what I wasn't prepared for was the frantic e-mail from Amari that came just a few short weeks after Christine and I had arrived back in Jerusalem...

Chapter Twenty-Three

"The Vision Is Snatched Away"

Late December, 1999:
In his e-mail, Amari anxiously explained that our sponsors had, for all intents and purposes, taken over the work. No longer would Christine and I be involved, he was told, but instead a young man from the Ukraine was assigned by the sponsors to oversee the entire work in Portgarad, Georgia, and Armenia. Amari would do the foot work but would be directly under this young man. Trying to understand what was going on, Amari stressed that this set-up could jeopardize the crucial network of backing and support we had received from the apostle in Armenia. Yevgeni's cooperation and assistance came as a result of a pre-existing trust relationship with Amari who in turn knew and trusted me, his American sister.

I couldn't believe what I was reading! When I communicated with our sponsors to inquire about all this, I was informed that Christine and I were no longer needed! I was crushed beyond words. It felt to me as if a kind of mutiny had just taken place and at the hands of my Christian brothers! After all, God had given me the vision. And Christine and I had sought out the sponsors who initially told us to keep accurate records and move out on the work as the Lord led. They would provide the finances and the framework to carry out the vision, but we would take the lead in its implementation. That was the original agreement! For me this all meant listening closely to the Holy Spirit's instructions and steering the ship at least for a season. But alas, I had been thrown overboard! I felt a little bit like Joseph in the pit when his jealous brothers wrenched his 'coat of many colors' off of him. And I have to admit that some of the things that the Lord later revealed to me in a dream seemed to explain the poor judgment of my brothers' actions in this way. There was a kind of jealousy coming from one quarter of the sponsorship that couldn't handle the fact that not only were events connected with setting up the aliyah moving ahead rapidly, but

153

God was using two ordinary women to help get the job done. The sponsors strategically held the purse strings. There was little I could do but trust God to protect the work that had been started and guard my own heart as I recognized that God is sovereign and that it's up to Him to judge and correct. I have to admit that the hurt from their actions seared the very bottom of my soul, but nonetheless it was up to me to forgive and release.

As I recall, I was able to get out one or two e-mails to Amari before the laptop that the sponsors had lent us was taken back. Fortunately and by the grace of God, because it was in Amari's heart to see God's work carried out above all else, (even if it meant submitting to this young man and system that had been superimposed), the aliyah work continued. After those initial contacts with Amari where I tried to soften and play down the severity of what had happened, I totally fazed myself out of the picture. That seemed like the best thing to do under the circumstances. In fact, at the Lord's bidding, I kept my hands totally off from the situation until just a few short weeks ago, (in early Spring of 2004), when, as I started writing this final chapter from Jerusalem, I was given the release to send an e-mail to Amari. In it I inquired about the status of the aliyah ministry and the little Jewish baby that Amari and Vera had adopted. What a thrill it was to immediately receive back a reply, complete with pictures of their little boy! Not only that, but I learned that the following day, (after sending my e-mail), the aliyah office in Portgarad was scheduled to be closed down. Had I not responded to the Holy Spirit's prompting when I did, I could have totally lost contact with Amari. So much time had elapsed since our last communication, (some four years), that the only way that I knew how to reach him was via the aliyah office e-mail address. That address was about to become history! Praise God for His nudge to make contact when I did. Of course I had no way of knowing all of this in the natural. But my Heavenly Father certainly knew, and it was within the framework of His perfect timing that He chose to reveal some wonderful news to me!

First of all let me say that this communication from Amari was like Holy Oil being poured over any remaining scars or wounds I might have carried from the untimely takeover by the sponsors. Somehow, his words brought not only closure to this particular chapter of my life, but it opened the door for something new as well. Yes, my part in God's vision had ended ever so abruptly, that's true. But whenever I glanced down at Amari's report and learned that over 1500 Jews had made aliyah to Israel through the work that had begun in Portgarad, my spirit leaped and rejoiced within me. The Lord God of Abraham, Isaac, and Jacob had indeed performed a mighty work! What He had begun, no man could stop. And then I looked down at the picture of Michael, the little Jewish baby we had found in the orphanage, the child that Amari and Vera had adopted. That was no less of a miracle! One day, I thought to myself...yes, one day soon, we will all meet here in Jerusalem. God will smile down on this event and what rejoicing there will be!

****

BUT the story isn't finished yet... no, not at all! There are new journeys to be walked out, and new chapters yet to be written as the Lord continues to unfold His marvelous plan of redemption for mankind, Jew and Gentile alike. It's all in the Book of Books you know! So for those who choose to believe, many adventures lie just ahead:

Adventures that by their very nature draw one into His Holy Presence, into that place where there must be, of necessity, an encounter...

An encounter that will transform your life forever...

An encounter with a "Supernatural God"!

POSTSCRIPT

"A Sudden Wind Shift to the West"

I've come to learn that doing it God's way means being sensitive to the Holy Spirit's timing. And so this current thrust to share my story is tied in with an urgent appeal to the church in North America to GET READY! Get ready to be God's vessel to help your Jewish brothers and sisters in a pending aliyah movement out of the WEST. "Out of the West," you may be asking? Yes, out of the West! Europe lies to the west of the tiny nation of Israel and so does North America. The United States alone has a population of more than six million Jews!

> *"Fear not, for I am with you;*
> *I will bring your descendants from the east,*
> *And gather you from the west;*
> *I will say to the north, 'Give them up!'*
> *And to the south, 'Do not keep them back!'*
> *Bring My sons from afar,*
> *And My daughters from the ends of the earth."*
> *(Isaiah 43:5&6)*

We've seen a rather massive aliyah come out of the old Soviet bloc countries, especially in the 1990s right after Perestroika and the fall of Communist Mother Russia. Likewise, right now before our very eyes we are watching scenes being played out that will lead up to the breakdown of America as we know it: near financial collapse, political chaos orchestrated by Big Government control, moral decline that wanes in comparison to the Biblical Sodom and Gomorrah, and a partial if not total 'turning the back' when it comes to Israel. Basically put, America is beyond broke, beaten down militarily, financially, and politically by its war on terror, and so misdirected from her original vision of a moral and godly Judeo-Christian nation that her eventual fall is not only pending, but in the minds of many God-fearing and Biblically prophetic voices, it is certain. Because of this, North American Jewry, (and especially the USA Jewish population, some six million strong), needs to turn their hearts towards the Jewish Homeland and make their aliyah NOW before it's too late! Today as I write they can leave America with their financial assets and safety intact. But as conditions in America continue to deteriorate, the American Jew will likely be faced with the fallout of anti-Semitism as well as his own practical and emotional survival.

ALL ROADS LEAD TO JERUSALEM would not be complete without a strong appeal to those readers who have 'ears to hear' what the Holy Spirit is saying about Israel, the times we are living in, and the call to pray, warn, and assist North American Jewry with the Biblical mandate to return to their Homeland. Perhaps you have been touched or inspired by this book, especially regarding how the Lord used ordinary people in the Russian, Georgian and Armenian churches to supernaturally implement and carry out the work of aliyah from their respective countries. Is it possible that your heart, too, is 'burning to help the Jews'?

You may recall from chapters eight and thirteen of this book that I referred back to a rather detailed four part dream that I had back in 1992. In these earlier chapters I told about seeing the port at Portgarad, Russia in my dream even before I arrived there in 1994! I also noted other scenes in that same dream that were realized during my time spent in Russia. Just the other day as I was working on this postscript, another segment of this same dream lit up in my spirit and I at last understood with more clarity something that was being said in the dream. The setting in this part of the dream was a smaller back room in some kind of fellowship or community building. The walls of the room were made of wood paneling and a small podium was in the front of the room. In the room were a number of ministry folks, including one man I knew who was known for his anointing to move in the prophetic. As this scene in my dream continued I became aware of two young men in the room who had been given prophetic words directly from God. I didn't know exactly what these prophetic words were, but as a 'voice' suddenly began to speak to all of us in the room I knew that this prophecy had something to do with my future ministry endeavors. In fact, everyone in the room seemed anxious to hear since this information also affected them for the same, or a similar, reason. The 'voice' said to, **"Watch the weather for a sudden wind shift to the WEST!"** The prophet in the room, (who also happened to be an airplane pilot and again someone that I knew in real life), made strong eye contact with me while these words were being spoken. His non-verbal communication alerted me to pay strong attention to what was being said. After that he left the room.......

The next day when I shared this dream 'in real life' with my pilot friend, he told me that for the pilot, a sudden wind shift to the west indicated that stormy weather was approaching. Not only are there major storms brewing politically and economically here in America right now, storms that could have dire consequences for both Jew and Christian, but this sudden wind shift to the 'west' will have a significant impact on Israel, the Middle East and the world. Just as 'Perestroika' resulted from a politically and economically bankrupt Russia hit by floods, drought, and famine to the degree that nearly half of Russia's hard currency was needed to purchase desperately needed food supplies for her masses, so the current American economic and political turbulence coupled with extreme weather conditions and rising food prices, has the potential to sow the seeds of hyperinflation and collapse. I might add also that the Russian-run Chernobyl nuclear plant accident in the Ukraine in April, 1986 was a major tipping factor that brought about Perestroika and conditions that left the 'pharaoh' of Russia at the time, Mikhail Gorbachev, no choice but to let God's people, the Jews, go! Is it possible that another toxic accident that took place in the Gulf of Mexico in April of 2010 has the potential to push America over the edge? Or, what about the potential for some kind of nuclear attack or accident? There's a lot of cover-up regarding the 2010 BP oil spill and the massive poisoning that has taken place in the Gulf region. Massive amounts of the highly toxic oil dispersant, Corexit, have been dumped on the waters of the Gulf. Our waters, our seafood, and our Gulf coast population have been poisoned. Watch for the 'fallout' from this hyper covered-up tragedy to impact millions of lives in the weeks and months ahead. Is it possible that this, or other ominous events, will break the spirit of 'mammon' which materialistically imprisons so many of America's Jews from desiring to return to their Jewish Homeland, Israel? **Will the Church be ready to do for the American Jew who desires to leave 'Egypt' what their Russian counterparts did for Soviet Jewry?** The answer to this question has eternal ramifications.

My prayer is that as the God of Israel supernaturally implanted a love for Israel and the Jewish people in the newly emerging Russian, Ukrainian, and Eastern European churches that were raised up after the collapse of Communism, that the same love and desire to pray for, warn, and assist North American Jewry will become supernaturally resident in the hearts of Christians throughout America and Canada. The call is out to vigilantly watch the shifting wind patterns to the WEST, recognizing that from all points of the globe, *"All Roads Lead To JERUSALEM", the place of His throne.* Yes, our Messiah Yeshua will rule and reign from this very throne as the sureness of His Word tells us. And, without a doubt, the sons and daughters of Abraham will be brought Home from the north, the south, the east and even the WEST. Get ready! It may just be that the Lord is preparing you or your congregation to help in a glorious aliyah effort from the west. God grant us all 'ears to hear' what the Spirit is saying during this awesome event of the second Exodus!

"In the Service of our 'Soon-Coming' King",
Harriot Hayes